Mary Magdalene

The Darker Saint

by

Claire Pingel

All rights reserved, no part of this publication may be reproduced or transmitted by any means whatsoever without the prior permission of the publisher.

Edited by Toni Glitz
glitzedit.co.uk

Text © Claire Pingel
Cover image © Lorenzo Pasinelli
Public Domain
ISBN: 979-8-341285-8-80

Veneficia Publications
August 2024

VENEFICIA PUBLICATIONS UK
veneficiapublications.com

DEDICATION

I would love to dedicate this book to two people. One who gave me life, and the other who is my life support.

My lovely mother, Dorothy, whom I lost in February 2023. She was a great encouragement to me and when I had doubts about my ability to write this book, she had true faith in me. My sadness is that I never got to tell her that I had done it, that I had finished.

The second person is my husband, Robert. He is my biggest cheerleader, and my Christos. Gentle, healing and wise.

CONTENTS

CHAPTER 1
AN AWAKENING _____ 1

CHAPTER 2
WHO WAS MARY MAGDALENE? _____ 7

CHAPTER 3
RELICS AND BLOODLINE _____ 11

CHAPTER 4
RELIGIOUS TEXTS _____ 42

CHAPTER 5
SYMBOLS RELATED TO MARY _____ 84

CHAPTER 6
THE ROLES OF THE MAGDALENE _____ 91

CHAPTER 7
SACRED SYMBOLS, FLOWERS
AND EPITHETS _____ 104

CHAPTER 8
MARY, THE DIVINE FEMININE _____ 121

CHAPTER 9
MARY IN THE ARTS AND MEDIA _____ 124

CHAPTER 10
THE MAGDALENE LAUNDRIES _____ 138

CHAPTER 11
MY OWN EXPERIENCES WITH MARY ___ 141

CHAPTER 12
PRACTICAL WORK _____ 151

CHAPTER 13
MAGDALENE MYSTERIES AND
NOVENAS _____ 157

CHAPTER 14
VISUALISATIONS AND MEDITATIONS __ 163

CHAPTER 15
PATHWORKING TO VISIT MARY _____ 174

CHAPTER 16
CONCLUSION _____ 181

CHAPTER 17
RECIPES _____ 183
FURTHER READING _____ i
REFERENCES _____ vii
ONLINE BIBLICAL REFERENCES _____ ix
IMAGES FEATURED _____ xii

CHAPTER 1
AN AWAKENING

It all began in 2015. I was lost. Then I was found. Mary Magdalene came into my life, she enlightened me and changed it beyond all recognition.

I started to investigate Paganism around 2001, following years of being disillusioned with the Christian Church. I began researching different branches of spirituality, starting with the usual introductory texts such as *White Magic* by Titania Hardie, followed by the Kate West series of books. There is a story here too. *White Magic* landed in my lap accidently. I was a member of a monthly book club which had an Editor's Choice that you had to cancel by returning a completed slip. If the book club did not hear from you, they posted the book out to you. Yes, you guessed it, I was busy and forgot to return the slip, and *White Magic* landed on my doorstep. I will admit here that I could not be bothered to return it, and after a few weeks of kicking myself that I never took it back to the Post Office, I decided to read it.

Years of child rearing and business development took over most of my time but slowly and surely, I continued seeking out knowledge, reading lots of witchcraft texts and putting into practice what I could, working as a solitary practitioner. So what changed in 2015? I had my spiritual awakening. It all started with a bout of athlete's foot. Yes, it really did! A foot fungus is responsible for who I am today.

My eldest child picked the foot malady up following a cadet swimming session in our local pool. I soon caught it from them.

I remember sitting in our local Greek café, eating polenta cake, looking down at my left foot, which was very swollen. It got bigger as the day went on. So, on returning home, I phoned the out-of-hours clinic, saw a doctor who diagnosed cellulitis and they gave me antibiotics the size of horse pills. And here is where things started to change. I took them four times a day as required, but a night time tablet changed my life. I wasn't sitting up properly, and I choked on it. I saw blue lights and was starting to pass out. It was terrifying but I managed to cough the tablet up. Long story short, I stopped taking all my medications, which included lifesaving ones and strong pain relief, and then stopped eating and drinking due to fear of choking again. As you can imagine, I became very unwell and ended up with multiple hospital admissions. This is where lines blur. Did I have a mental condition, was it withdrawal from the medications, or was I physically unwell? Looking back now, I think it was my spiritual awakening.

As I started to recover, my husband, who had looked after me and stood by me through this most trying time, took me on several trips to Glastonbury, as this was what my heart was crying out for. I look back at selfies taken at the Chalice Well, and I can see the pain and fear in my eyes. I tried to walk up the Tor but was too weak. But this episode reawakened the stirrings of my love for the Goddess deep within my soul, which I had previously suppressed due to the mundane aspects of life taking over.

So, during my recovery, I made the commitment to seek out moots and groups in my local area. I also bought lots of books and started devouring the knowledge contained in them. I called myself Wiccan, even though at that time I was neither initiated nor in a coven. I found a traditionalist witchcraft coven around 2018 and spent a few short months there. The High Priestess asked me to leave due to health concerns, as I still wasn't really back to my normal self. I was understandably devastated but rather than giving up or taking time out to heal, I started going to Pagan camps and saw an advert for a local Fellowship of Isis group. This was run by my local moot leader. So I applied, and part of the learning process was to work with, and develop a relationship with, three Goddesses of my choice.

I selected Isis as my first choice. This was an easy choice to make, being a long-standing fan of Ancient Egypt ever since I had worked on a school project; my house is filled with Egyptian replica statues. My second choice was Cerridwen. I tried so hard to have a fulfilling spiritual relationship with her; I studied and researched her, but I could only manage surface-level interaction.

My third choice was initially Hestia. I found my interaction with her even harder, and even though I now sometimes work with Hestia as part of Orphic rituals I attend, I still don't have a close bond with her. But somewhere in the background was a great pull. It's hard to describe, but there was a Divine Feminine energy in the background trying to get my attention. I had a short dabble with Oya but there was still not a massive bond.

I researched all these Goddesses deeply, but none called to my heart and soul. Next was Hekate. Now I have a big bond with her and magically work as a Hekatean witch. She became my second Goddess, as I continued working with Isis. I also work with Santa Muerte, Lilith And Sulis Minerva but none of them called as strongly. There was another voice coming from deep inside. meditated and focused on who was calling my name.

During this time, my family encountered a group of people who held firm patriarchal Christian values.

A woman's voice from deep within started shouting *What about me?* It felt like I needed to hear this strong female Christian voice, calling from deep inside. A suppressed voice, driven out by the patriarchy, wanting, needing to be noticed. Documentaries started appearing on the television, random adverts on my Facebook pages, and friend requests from Priestesses.

When it all finally slotted into place, I had already joined a Wiccan coven and had to order a set book. Next to the book I had to order, was a book on Mary Magdalene and I was so drawn to this book, that I had to have it. I read it from cover to cover, before the Coven book.

This is where my love affair with the divine feminine energy I now know as Mary Magdalene began. It has not stopped, in fact, my interactions and love for this Goddess of divine spiritual energy have continuously increased. The more I research the Magdalene and different people's experiences with her, the more abundantly clear it becomes that she arrives in the devotee's life just at the right time, when she is needed the most. At times of struggle, depression, and adversity. Because of the challenges Mary went through, the fear and devastation she suffered, she has an innate ability to support, and just hold us when we open ourselves up to her. We need to trust that she knows what's best for us; she is a role model and a divine energy source – an archetype for our modern times.

CHAPTER 2
WHO WAS MARY MAGDALENE?

Mary Magdalene, is also known as Miryam of Magdala and is highly likely to be the person referred to in The Bible as Mary of Bethany. She was born into the prestigious Tribe of Benjamin just over two thousand years ago, possibly in the town of Magdala, along the shoreline of Galilee, in Israel. Her noble parents were Syrus and Eucharia and she was the sister of Martha and Lazarus, who was famously restored to life by Jesus.

Nowhere in the New Testament does it say that Mary is from Magdala in Israel; this is an educated guess by scholars. She could have come from Egypt, where there was a town called Magdolum, or even from a place called Magdala in Southern Ethiopia – this village is currently called Amba Mariam, (Fort Mary). How curious that a village previously known as Magdala is now called Amba Mariam.

The name Magdala is Aramaic for tower or fortress, whereas the Hebrew word M'gdal also means pillar or watchtower – the kind that shepherds used to watch over their flocks – or it could simply mean that she took the name from the village of Magdala, along the shores of the sea of Galilee. This has caused speculation that she led the Flock of Israel, but there is no historical evidence to back this up.

Mary Magdalene is named twelve times in the New Testament, which is more than any other woman in the New Testament, and in fact, more than most of the twelve male apostles. There is some confusion over the number of different Marys mentioned, as the name Mary – and other forms of the name Mary, such as Maryam and Miriam – were common names within the Jewish community during that time. Other notable Marys include Mother Mary and Mary of Clopas, who is thought to be the aunt of Jesus. We cannot be certain that Mary Magdalene and Mary of Bethany are the same person, but my personal belief is that she is. The Eastern Orthodox Church sees Mary Magdalene and Mary of Bethany as two different people.

Mary Magdalene is mentioned in all four of the canonical gospels: Matthew, Mark, Luke, and John. Each gospel tells roughly the same story but from a different person's perspective. They originated in the oral tradition and were written from the memories of the Disciples between thirty-five and sixty-five years after the death of Jesus. The Gospels of Matthew, Mark, and Luke date to around 65–85 CE and the stories are more closely related to each other than the Gospel of John which is more mystical and was written around 90–95 CE. Mary's stories in the Gospels generally relate to the passion of Jesus, his death around the year 30 CE, and then his resurrection.

The passion story details the period from Jesus's arrest through to his crucifixion. In fact, there are so many women with the name Mary, that there have been suggestions that Mary, Maryam, and Miriam could actually be a title given to Priestesses. It was a role you would be initiated into and, according to the Dead Sea Scrolls, Mary is the title given to healers. This would explain why there were Marys of towns and regions, for example, Mary of Bethany could mean a Priestess of Bethany.

Mary Magdalene as a Priestess of Isis

Some historical accounts say that around the age of 11–12 (although these are estimates) Mary Magdalene left Israel for Egypt to become a devotee of Isis and serve as a Priestess in the Temple of Isis. Here she learned the secrets of sacred femininity, sex magic and sexual alchemy. She became skilled in the death rites of Egyptian temples and studied the cycle of life, death, and rebirth.

This put her in good stead for her future role, that of anointing the King of the Jews. There is evidence of her Priesthood in the gospels too, with the anointing of Jesus, and the preparation of his body after death, both of which are part of Priestess training. There are mentions in The Talmud, of Jesus being trained in Egyptian magic, too.

Several years later, Mary was sent back to Israel to spread her knowledge, and this is where she could have met Jesus.

There is speculation that Mary was initially married to John the Baptist and that they lived in a type of commune; a spiritual camp run by him. John taught rebirth by full body baptism in the river Jordan, and taught the old ways of the solar and lunar mysteries. The story goes that John and Mary had fallen in love, married and Mary gave birth to a son, also named John. It was a difficult marriage. When Jesus arrived at the camp it was clear to John that there was a connection between Mary and Jesus, so he released Mary to be with her new beloved. I have only seen this story mentioned once in all my research, so I cannot verify its source.

CHAPTER 3
RELICS AND BLOODLINE

There is speculation that Jesus and Mary were married and that the anointing was an act of marriage, as well as the making of a King. The anointing could also have been an enactment of rites from a fertility cult in the ancient Middle East, a form of hieros gamos – the royal bride who anoints the king. Because they touched each other in public, which was illegal under Judaic Law at the time, it is a possibility that needs to be considered.

Nowhere in the Bible does it say Jesus was unmarried, or celibate, or give any reasons at all for his bachelorhood. Also, they were both thought to be in their thirties when they met, and to remain single at that age was unusual in Israel at that period in history. It was a stigma to be single, deviating from Jewish tradition, surely this fact would be mentioned somewhere in the biblical texts? If they had in fact been married, Jesus from the royal House of David and Mary from the powerful Tribe of Benjamin would have made a powerful political and regal union. There is also speculation that she was carrying a child at the time of Jesus's death, and this may have been the reason for her fleeing Israel by boat, for sanctuary, for the safety of herself and her unborn child. Historians have suggested that Mary gave birth to a baby girl named Sarah.

There is some loosely based evidence that Mary, her sister Martha, and her brother Lazarus, along with Joseph of Arimathea travelled to the UK around the year 40 CE. There are differing accounts as to who was on the boats; some say that a servant girl called Sarah, Mary Salome (mother of the Apostles James and John), Mary Jacobi (Mother Mary's sister) and even St. Maximin (the first Bishop of Provence) who pops up later in Mary's story, may have accompanied her. They fled quickly, possibly because they were protecting Mary. They could have been persecuted and fled for their lives, hunted by the authorities – the Romans – and had to go into hiding to protect loved ones.

Immediately after the death of Jesus, Christianity was declared illegal, and punishable by death. The boat they used was in a terrible state, rudderless, oarless, and had no sail. Was this boat sabotaged, or did they grab the first available boat? We know Mary was wealthy, and so was Joseph of Arimathea. He owned the burial tomb that Jesus had laid in. They could have afforded a better boat, so time must have been against them.

They were thought to have called at the Scottish Isles of Mull and Iona, before travelling on to Glastonbury, where Glastonbury Abbey has a Virgin Mary Chapel built around 63 CE by Joseph. He said he was guided by Archangel Gabriel to build a Chapel on this site and along with twelve of his followers, he built the rustic chapel from wattle and daub. The foundations of this chapel were discovered beneath St. Joseph's crypt at the abbey. Joseph is believed to be buried in the Abbey grounds.

The holy thorn on Wearyall Hill in Glastonbury is thought to have originated from the staff of Joseph of Arimathea. It is said that after climbing the hill he decided to rest and thrust his staff into the ground and took a well-earned rest. When he awoke the next morning, the staff had rooted. Known as the holy thorn, it is unusual in that it flowers twice a year, Easter time and Christmas time – the two holiest times of the year.

It is a hawthorn tree, but not a native hawthorn, it is a middle eastern variety, that flowers and bears berries at the same time.

There are remains of a Magdalene Chapel in Glastonbury on Bride's Mound to the West of the Town. The group who travelled to Britain are speculated to have brought the Holy Grail with them and buried it below the Tor at the entrance to the underworld, and the water and spring at the Chalice Well are thought to flow from the Grail. The lion's head drinking fountain at the Chalice Well Gardens is said to depict the Lion of Judah and the sacred bloodline of the Holy Grail. Jesus is known as the Lion of Judah as he was descended from the Tribe of Judah, through David and Solomon, one of the twelve tribes of Israel. The lion is the strongest and therefore the leader or king.

The Lion's Head Fountain at the Chalice Well Glastonbury

After the visit to the UK, the group sailed across the channel to France, landing near Marseille in the Provence region. Martha went to Avignon, and Lazarus stayed in Marseille.

Mary remained in Marseille, staying with Lazarus for a short while, finding sanctuary amongst the Jewish community. She found it unsettling and difficult at first but with the support of this community, she eventually settled. Mary was revered as royalty, as the child she gave birth to was descended from Jewish kings, namely David and Solomon, and the noble Tribe of Benjamin.

Her daughter, Sarah, was brought up in France. Sarah was the start of the royal lineage of Mary and Jesus, which later was thought to have become the bloodline of the Merovingian kings of France.

Chapelle du Sainte Pilon

Mary spent her time spreading the teachings of Jesus, and after many years of teaching, her latter years were spent in penance and prayer. This theory is generally accepted by historians, although it is unclear what the penance was for. She ended her days some thirty years later.

She had lived in a cave near Sainte-Baume, where it is said she was given Holy Communion each day by visiting Angels. The Golden Legend text written by a 13th century Italian Dominican monk called Jacques de Voragine, states that when she neared death, four angels carried her to the top of the Sainte-Baume Mountain seven times a day to receive spiritual ecstasy and food. To mark this place, there now stands the Magdalene dedicated chapel of Saint Pilon (pilon means pillar) which was built in 1618. The chapel had replaced a pillar that had a statue on it of Mary Magdalene which had been dedicated to her in 1493. Something interesting to note here, is the name, Caves of Sainte-Baume. Baume means balm, and Mary had the alabaster jar of nard oil balm. Could the caves have been named due to this connection?

The French locals tell a different story, however. They believe that Mary was driven out of Israel as she was gathering too many followers and becoming a threat to the religious beliefs endemic in the region, so she was put out to sea with her brother and sister, Lazarus, Martha and two other Marys in a boat with no rudders, oars or sails.

Three Marys are reminiscent of the triple Goddess, and there are three Marys mentioned in the Gnostic Gospel of Philip (Nag Hammadi texts) who were said to be constant companions of Jesus. The boat washed up on the shores of Saintes-Maries-de-la-Mer (named after her) near Provence. They travelled such great distances with an imperfect boat, it is almost like they had the protection of Jesus with them. She had to put a lot of faith into that rickety boat. She preached to and taught the locals her wisdom. She became beloved to them and was named Saint Mary Magdalene, the Goddess of Christianity.

Mary's Relics

Mary's body lies in rest in Saint-Maximin-la-Sainte-Baume and most of her relics remain there. Her skull is held in a reliquary covered with bronze angels, and some of her remains are in a sarcophagus.

Reliquary housing the skull of Mary Magdalene

The story around Mary's remains is not a straightforward one. Around 860 AD, a monk named Baudillon brought relics, thought to be the bones of Mary Magdalene, to Vézelay in the heart of France from Saint-Maximin-la-Sainte-Baume. In 1058, almost two centuries later, the pope declared these relics to be authentic, and groups of pilgrims began to visit the site.

The site soon became established as an important place of pilgrimage, bringing money to the local area. The building of the Basilica of La Madeleine was started in 1096 to house the relics. The decline of Vézelay as a pilgrimage site was linked with the discovery of a body, presumed to be that of Mary, in 1279 at Sainte-Maximin-la-Sainte-Baume in Provence. The relics in Vézelay were subsequently destroyed by the Protestant Huguenots who burnt them in the 16th century, but the location still remains a pilgrimage site for the faithful, and they do have a few small bones from the new discovery in a reliquary shaped like the Ark of the Covenant.

Mary's remains were found in Sainte-Maximin-la-Sainte-Baume by Charles the Second of Naples. He had been researching Mary, trying to ascertain whether she was buried in the area. Charles had discovered accounts that Saint-Maximin had buried her body in the town that bore his name.

An excerpt from a diary entry made by a chronicler on 9th December 1279, notes that Charles was excavating the crypt of the Church of Sainte-Maximin-la-Sainte-Baume. The translations of the entry read as follows.

> ... the prince had stripped his chlamyde (cape), and armed with a hoe, he dug the earthe with such ardor that he was inundated with sweat, those who were there met a marble tomb work ...

Charles found a stone coffin bearing the name of Saint Sidoine and with it was a parchment with a Latin inscription, translated as follows.

> The year of the Nativity of the Lord 710, 6th day of December, at night and very secretly, under the reign of the very pious Eudes, King of the French, at the time of the ravages of the treacherous Saracen nation,

this body of the very dear and venerable Saint Marie Madeleine was, for fear of the treacherous nation, transferred from Her alabaster tomb to this marble tomb, after having removed Sidoines body from it, because it was better hidden there.

The tomb was sealed back up until the following May (1280), when a large group of dignitaries gathered outside. The seal was broken, and the tomb reopened. Among the relics was a wax seal stating in Latin, *Hic requiescit corpus Mariae Magdalenae* – Here lies the body of Mary Magdalene.

Her relics were almost complete, with the exception of one leg and the lower jaw, which were missing. There was some hair in place and, miraculously, a small piece of flesh above her left browbone where Jesus was thought to have touched her on the day of his resurrection as in the following bible quote.

> Jesus said to her, "Do not cling to me, for I have not yet ascended to the Father; but go to my brothers and say to them, 'I am ascending to my Father and your Father, to my God and your God'."
> John 20: 17

There was also a small amphora found next to Mary's remains that was thought to contain earth stained with the blood of Jesus. Unfortunately, this went missing in 1904.

In 1283 her skull was placed into the reliquary in the Basilica of Maximin-la-Sainte Baume. The small piece of flesh was placed in a vial under the skull, and is known as the *noli me tangere*, which is Latin and means 'touch me not'. In 1295 a Basilica was built under the orders of the Pope.

Mary's relics are paraded around the streets on her feast day, July 22nd, in a golden mask covering her blackened skull and some kind of wig. Analysis of her skull and hair in 1974 indicated the remains were of a female aged around 50 years of Mediterranean descent. The Catholic Church will not allow any part of the skull to be removed for dating, so her year of death has not been determined.

Mary's left foot was rediscovered in 2000 after being lost for centuries and is now in a silver foot-shaped reliquary in the Basilica of St. John the Baptist of the Florentines (Basilica of San Giovanni dei Fiorentini) just across the river from the Vatican. It had originally been given as a gift to the pope.

Mary's left hand is in the Simonopetra Monastery in Greece and one of her teeth is in the Metropolitan

Museum of Art in New York City. Her hand, the Myrrophores hand, is intact, enclosed in a reliquary and is said to give off the smell of precious oils with some claiming to feel warmth from it. The hand is linked to miracles, it is said to have held back fire, stopped worms from eating plants and made a swarm of locusts disappear.

According to the Eastern tradition, Mary is not buried in France at all, but in Ephesus, where she died and was buried after accompanying St. John the Apostle.

Vézelay Basilica
The church is also known as the Basilica of Sainte-Marie-Madeleine and was constructed between 1120 and 1150, replacing a 9th century abbey. Built in the style of Burgundian Romanesque art, it is now a UNESCO World Heritage site, having been added to the list in 1979 due to its outstanding architecture and history in relation to medieval Christianity.

On the 24th of June at midday, when the sun is at its zenith, the sun's rays stream in through the window at the centre of the nave and a path of light forms nine individual shining pools which light up along the aisle, perfectly aligned with the tiles on the ground, to celebrate the feast day of John the Baptist. The altar is bathed in sunlight. It truly is a feat of sacred geometry, it is aligned with waterways and the electromagnetic energy lines running under the church and it is also interesting to note that the crypt holds a few bones of Mary. This phenomenon happens for the whole of June, so it includes the summer solstice. At the winter solstice the light rays illuminate the pillars, so perfect stripes glow across the same floor.

There is a narrow staircase carved into the rock leading down to the crypt. On the back wall, behind the railings, where the bones are kept, there is wallpaper with the ascension symbol of the flower of life printed onto it.[1]

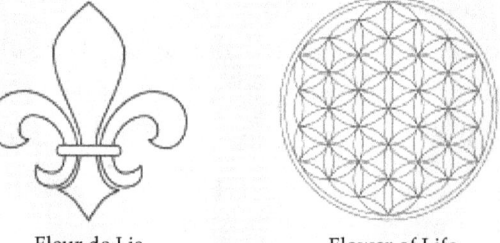

Fleur de Lis   Flower of Life

There are also fleur-de-lis, the symbol of the Merovingians on this wallpaper. The few bones here (said to be rib bone fragments) are contained in a replica of the Ark of the Covenant, and a pillar has a circular reliquary containing a tiny bone shard.

---

[1] The flower of life is an ancient sacred geometry symbol made up of full circles that overlap each other to form the representation of a flower.. It is said to represent the cycle of creation.

There is a 12th-century tympanum above the central door of the original part of the church. Jesus is seated, surrounded by his disciples. His arms are outstretched, but his left hand is missing, having been chopped off during one of the wars. His left hand! The left hand identifies with the Feminine. The female attributes include caring for others, trusting our own wisdom, compassion and community for example. All attributes that Mary displays.

In a basilica devoted to Mary Magdalene it would appear that someone is trying to show that Jesus is incomplete without his beloved and it is indicative of the treatment of her by the Church throughout two millennia of Christianity.

There is a statue of Mary in the church depicting her holding what has been perceived as the holy grail to her stomach, instead of an alabaster jar. She has a knowing smile on her face and her eyes are downcast. The way she is holding the grail, with her hands in a protective stance guarding her stomach, drawing

Statue in the Basilique de Sainte Marie Madeleine

attention to that area, could be interpreted as her carrying the holy bloodline, although this is of course just a suggestion and highly speculative. I can find no record of the stonemason or sculptor of this statue, so I am assuming it was made at the same time that the basilica was built. This is the only image I can find of Mary in a basilica named after her – the tympanum is documented many more times than the statue, and the tympanum also seems to be the main architectural feature in the basilica.

Mary's Daughter Sarah/Sarah La Kali
The name Sarah means noblewoman or princess. She is known amongst the Romany people (who revere her as a patron saint) and the people of the Provence region as Sarah La Kali, Sarah the Black and Sarah the Egyptian. Kali is a Goddess from Northern India, where the Romany people originate.[2]

Sarah's annual feast day is celebrated on 25th May and thousands of Romany devotees converge on this area for the celebrations. Known as the French Convention, they form a parade, including men in costume on white horses, and take the statue of Sarah down to the sea,

---

[2] https://travellermovement.org.uk/gypsy-roma-and-traveller-history-and-culture.
This page is written by advocates of the Roma and traveller communities and describes their background and culture.

where a ritual is performed which includes dipping her into the water, similar to a holy bath in the Ganges river. Is this Sarah the daughter of Mary? Was this a different Sarah? Legends put her as a servant to the group that arrived on the boat from Israel. A church in Southern France dating from the 9th century has a shrine for a girl named Sarah. Is this Mary's daughter or the servant girl? Some scholars think that this Sarah was indeed the servant girl brought from the holy land, whereas others believe she is the daughter of Jesus and Mary.

The statue has dark skin, what we would now call a Black Madonna or Black Virgin. Near Sarah's black Madonna there is an image of Kali in a glass cabinet. Although the Roma deny worshipping Kali, they say that the word Kali in Romani means dark.

Sarah La Kali black Madonna

Black Madonnas
These have traditionally been found at Pagan sites of worship – Isis, Demeter, Cybele, Inanna and Diana are goddesses who have all at some time or another been depicted with black skin. In the past, lunar and earth goddesses have been depicted as dark to

differentiate them as feminine, with the sun and masculine portrayed as light, this was common in early Mediterranean civilisations. Some are called Black Earth Mother Goddess, as a Paganistic form of the black Madonna.

The Cult of Isis had reached France, and worship was likely to have been linked with the black Madonna. Paris was originally called Para Isidos (near Isis), and Notre Dame Cathedral was built on the site of an Isis cult temple. Isis shares some links with Mary, in that they are both linked with boats, and Isis was mourning her lost love, Osiris, just as Mary was mourning hers. Isis and Mary both bore a child after the death of their sacrificed grooms. The statuary is usually the same as the Madonna with or without her child, except the statues are black, that is black faces and hands. The images are usually heavily venerated, more so than the Catholic virgin and child images.

As well as the Saint Sarah black Madonna, there are at least three more in the Marseilles region, all in churches with links to Mary Magdalene, and two in the Cathar region of Montségur. There are almost four hundred black Madonna shrines around the world and approximately half of them are in Southern France. There are hills called the Monts de la Madeleine (Magdalene's Hills) in the areas of Vichy and Lyon that have many black Madonnas. Although these statues are clearly of Mary Magdalene and not Mother Mary, there is a curiosity here. They are mother and child, not the Madonna alone, almost a visual confirmation that Mary did indeed have a child.

To date, none of the Black Madonnas have been officially recognised by the Church, nor has their adoration been encouraged. One reason for this lack of recognition could be that the statues represent Mary Magdalene. A parish priest who was asked about the Black Madonna that had been displayed in his church for five hundred years, said it was an accumulation of dirt over the centuries and from candle smoke. Either he needs to sack his church cleaner or look more closely at the painted hands and face on the statue.

Why is the Church so bothered about a bit of paint? Could it be that the statue is black because the actual Madonna was black? Could it be the Pagan links which the Church is upset about? Numerous churches are built on old Pagan sites, such as temples or holy wells.

Some Black Madonnas were worshipped as dark Goddesses, the face of the crone, associated with hidden wisdom, the Sophia. Black could mean hidden in the darkness, the hidden nature of the sacred feminine; the dark, black, penitent life of the Magdalene in contrast to the whiteness of the Virgin Madonna. Mary is displayed as a Black Madonna at Chartres, France, entitled *Our Lady under the Earth*, suggestive of the hidden secrets. There are many more around France and into Spain that are said to represent Mary Magdalene.

Margaret Starbird, in her book *The Goddess in the Gospels*, suggests that this quote from the Song of Songs 1, refers to the Black Madonnas, and therefore links to Mary Magdalene. She suggests that Mary is the Bride in the Song of Songs.

The Goddess Mary Magdalene

"I am black and beautiful, O daughters of Jerusalem, like the tents of Kedar, like the curtains of Solomon. Do not gaze at me because I am dark, because the sun has gazed on me. My mother's sons were angry with me; they made me keeper of the vineyards, but my own vineyard I have not kept!"

Pagan Sites in the region
Mary's cave was thought to have been a centre of Isis worship around the time of her arrival in France. Near Mary's cave in Sainte Baume, was a site where the Goddess Diana Lucifera was worshipped, in the forest

of Diana. Mary is said to have preached the early form of Christianity outside a Pagan temple dedicated to Diana in Marseille, and she was not chased away by the Priestesses. Mary was more tolerated by the Priestesses than she had ever been by Simon Peter, although rumour had it that she may have been arrested there for heresy.

It is entirely possible that Mary was teaching her own edited version of old Pagan traditions, with some of the early Christian teachings thrown in which, let's face it, seem somewhat Pagan, with teachings of visions and soul progression.

This Mary that we now see in France, preaching outside temples, is a different Mary from the one in the New Testament. She has matured, and come out of her shell. Awakened and arisen. A survivor, no longer submissive. A profoundly powerful leader and teacher in her own right.

She was teaching the mystical teachings, the kind that were left out of the Bible and were hidden deep inside the Apocrypha gospels, which wasn't too far removed from what was being taught in the Pagan temples – remember here too that Mary was temple trained herself.

Near Mary's cave, hidden away, there is a cave called Grotte aux Oeufs (the cave of eggs). It's a narrow yoni-shaped cave, a place of the sacred feminine. It is quite difficult to find, the path is narrow, rocky and has some steep falls.

Top Left the entrance to the Cave of Mary Magdalene bottom left inside the cave and right the Cave of Eggs

Arles, in Provence, was a cult centre for Isis in antiquity. Alet-les-Bains (the chosen place) had two temples, one for Athena and one for Artemis. Minerve was named after Minerva and was an important Cathar city. A centre of Goddess worship in pre-Christian times.

Saintes-Maries-de-la-Mer had a Temple of Ra two thousand years ago, along with a cult of Isis in the region.

Domrémy-la-Pucelle is a small village in the Lorraine region where Joan of Arc grew up. Two kilometres away in a field is the Fairy tree, where she received her first calling. It is a site linked with sacred feminine worship and there was an ancient Celtic settlement here.

Saintes-Maries-de-la-Mer is in the Camargue region where the Mediterranean and Rhone river meet. Provence, in Mary's time, was part of the Roman Empire. A beautiful thriving, popular area, known for its pink flamingos and wild white horses.

The Merovingians
The Merovingian Kings of France were said to have been descended from the royal bloodline of Mary and Jesus and their emblem was the fleur-de-lis. The name derives from Mary and the Vine.

> The vineyard of the LORD Almighty is the nation of Israel, and the people of Judah are the vines he delighted in.
>
> Isiah 5: 7

Against the wishes of the Church of Rome, the kings were exceptionally tolerant of the Jewish community, who held high-ranking posts. Some of the kings were also given Jewish names, which was not normal at the time in France.

In 496 CE, the Church appeared to have accepted that the Merovingians were of divine blood, and made a pact with the kings, who were offered high-ranking roles within the Church. But as expected, the Church betrayed them and killed off King Dagobert II in the hopes of killing off the bloodline. With the Catholic Church being built around a divinity premise, they wanted people to believe that Jesus was divine, not human and therefore could not have a mortal bloodline. But King Dagobert had a son, Sigebert III who escaped, so it is probable that there are Merovingian descendants to this day.

The Merovingians were a mysterious bunch linked to strange phenomena, sometimes called the sorcerer kings, and were thought to have dabbled in the occult. Chronicles of the time suggested that they had healing gifts that were thought to have come from their blood; they could heal using the power of touch, for example. The Merovingians were thought to have all had a birthmark over their hearts, marking them as different and special. Could it be possible that they inherited the power of miracles through their holy lineage?

In 751, the Pope feared the power of the Merovingians. He called them Pagans, renounced them under the 'Donation of Constantine', exiled them to a monastery, and replaced them with the Carolingian dynasty, of which Charlemagne was a member.

The Donation of Constantine is an 8th century document, claiming to be from the 4th century, that was said to record Roman Emperor Constantine the Great bestowing vast territory and spiritual power over to Pope Sylvester 1 and his successors as a thank you for Pope Sylvester curing Emperor Constantine of leprosy. The document was declared a forgery in the 15th century by Lorenzo Valla but had been used by several Popes as a document of power.

The Knights Templar
The fighting monks, also known as The Order of the Poor Knights of Christ and the Temple of Solomon, the Knights Templar were a Catholic military order; the elite forces of their day, which operated for around two hundred years. The Templar's headquarters were luxurious lodgings at the ruins of King Solomon's temple mount in Jerusalem.

A Crusader Knight

They were the archetypal Crusader knights who fought and died in the name of Jesus. The Order was founded in 1118 by Hugues de Payens with eight other knights. One of their official functions was to protect pilgrims visiting the city, their white robes with a red cross on them being a familiar sight.

Unofficially they were thought to have been tasked with looking after the Ark of the Covenant, the Holy Grail, and other special items, moving them to safety as and when required, and excavating through the rubble and ruins of the holy land for secret documents.

They were a wealthy Order, owning land, and they had a banking system, as new recruits signed all their wealth over to the Order's coffers. This was at odds with their living a monk's lifestyle; they were not allowed possessions, and their daily life was heavily regulated having sworn oaths of poverty, chastity and obedience.

The order held the feminine in great reverence. Bernard of Clairvaux, a founding member and devotee of Black Madonnas, preached sermons on Mary of Bethany, some of which were in Vézelay. Their churches tended to be round, celebrating the pregnant Goddess, but after the suppression of the Templars, the building of round churches was banned. On Friday 13th (yes this is one of the reasons why people think this date is unlucky) 1307,

King Phillippe IV of France attacked the Templars, torturing and killing the leaders and imprisoning the rest of the Knights, on multiple charges, including heresy.

Interestingly some of the knights confessed to worshipping an idol they called Baphomet but not the goat-headed God that many of us know of. They described Baphomet as a blackened woman's skull from Egypt, covered in silver, with two cranial bones wrapped first in white linen and then in red linen. I can't help but think of the current relic of Mary; a blackened skull, encased in gold. Other knights talked, under torture, of worshipping the head of John the Baptist. Whether the relic, or a copy of the relic it is unclear. Also under duress, claims of secret ceremonies were revealed involving spitting and trampling on a cross.

It is likely that some of the Templars visited a church of John of the East which inspired their unusual underground practices. Could this be the religious commune where Jesus and Mary potentially met?

There is still a Tribe of Arabs in Nasiriya that revere John the Baptist and a dark Goddess Ruha, who they see as a holy spirit which appears in the form of a dove, like the Shekinah. The Tribe had slowly emigrated over from Egypt, escaping different persecutions along the way.

They see John as the High King of Light, they are Gnostic and their teachings are like Pistis Sophia. They loathe Jesus, calling him Yeshu, the lying Messiah.

When the Templars asked for forgiveness, for the Absolution of their sins, these were part of the words they would say, seeing Mary Magdalene as a symbol of redemption.

> I pray God that he will pardon you your sins as he pardoned them to St. Mary Magdalene and the thief who was put on the cross.

The Cathars
Also known as the Albigenses, they were very religious, holy people who lived in the Languedoc region of Southern France from the 10th – 14th century. They were Christians, who followed the teachings of Mary Magdalene and early Christianity.

Their ancestors had been evangelized by Mary and they had continued with their beliefs of a primitive pre-Roman Church. The teachings were Gnostic in nature, hating the hierarchy, including icons and images. Life on earth was seen as purgatory and to be free of the body was their wish. Many, after undertaking the consolamentum pre-death rites, took the Endura rites of self-induced starvation or even poison when faced with arrest.

The Cathars were healers and incredibly kind people, with their Church being called the Church of Love (Amor). The Church members believed that every person was a vessel – a holy grail – and could be filled with the holy spirit and be enlightened by God. They were against war and completely refused any form of violence, including the killing of animals, as God was within all creation.

Seeing themselves as preachers of the word of God, they believed in a dualistic universe where good battled evil. Evil was the creator of the world we live in, so the only way to redeem ourselves was to follow the teachings. They were loved and supported by the communities they lived in and when the Roman Catholic Church accused them of heresy and tried to persecute them around 1209, the local Roman Catholics protected them. Even when the towns were attacked, they, the Catholics, stayed steadfast; they loved the Cathars, and had given them the name Cathars, which comes from the Greek word for pure. Those in the area who were not Cathar were Cathar sympathisers, and it was almost a Cathar state. It was known as the Albigensian Crusade, and as the Catholic Church knew the Cathars loved Mary, they started the attacks on her feast day, July 22nd, 1209, at Béziers in South-Western France. So, we have Christians murdering other Christians, protected by some Christians in a Christian country on the orders of the

Pope. There were 15,000 – 20,000 ordinary people killed, with around 200 of them being Cathars. The townsfolk had been given the chance to leave but wouldn't hand over the Cathars, so they were all executed.

The Roman Catholic Inquisition started in this region before it went to Spain, and those who survived these attacks were questioned. They told the Church that they followed *The Gospel of the Beloved Companion*, which the Church interpreted as the apostle John's Gospel. It does share a lot of synchronicities with the Gospel of John and a lot of similarities with the Gospel of Thomas. But we now know that it was the Gospel of Mary, which had also been translated into the Cathar language of Occitan. It is thought that Mary brought the documents with her when she sailed from the holy land.

There was an 11th century monk called Rabanus Maurus who wrote a book called *De Laudibus Sanctae Crucis*, which tells of Mary being banished from Israel after the crucifixion and landing in France with several documents thought to have been written in Greek.

There have been many historical documents throughout the Middle Ages and later which say the Cathars are the holders of Mary Magdalene's secrets. There was *The Gospel of The Beloved Companion*, translated from Greek and published by Jehanne de Quillan, which claims to be the complete Gospel of Mary Magdalene, as opposed to the fragmented copy found in Upper Egypt, and was thought to have been protected by the community in France that Jehanne lived in.

There was a legend that just before the Roman Catholics finally got hold of the Cathars, four of them escaped to the mountain of Montségur in Languedoc and hid these precious documents there. But was it really just documents? Whatever it was, it took four Cathars to carry. Some theorise that they took the holy grail up there along with documents. Four people went, but how many came back? If less than four, they may have hidden the *sangraal* (holy grail bloodline) there. It was not money bags, as the Cathar's wealth had been accounted for. They were not materialistic people, so whatever it was had to be of great importance – their most cherished secret. This led to speculation that it was the Ark of the Covenant that they hid.

There was an interesting prophecy made in 1321, by a Guillaume Béilbaste. He was a Cathar Perfect, a leader, who could undertake rituals for his community. There was a ritual called the consolamentum which is similar to the last rites, a death ritual. He had escaped and was in hiding in Northern Spain and was tricked into coming out of hiding, by being told there was a Cathar woman near death who wanted these rites performed for her. He was captured by the Inquisitors and sentenced to be burned at the stake. Before his death, he shouted that in seven hundred years the laurel would be green again. The Cathars were closely linked to the laurel tree, so he predicted the return of the Cathar beliefs, the Church of Love and the return of the Magdalene. Seven hundred years was 2021. The time is now.

> I tell you this: when all have abandoned me, only she shall stand beside me like a tower. A tower built on a high hill and fortified cannot fall, nor can it be hidden. From this day forth, she shall be known as Migdalah, for she shall be as a tower to my flock, and the time will soon come when her tower shall stand alone by mine.
> Gospel of the Beloved Companion

This is significant. Jesus recognised Mary as a tower. A tower of strength. Something she needed to be, given the challenges she faced. She wasn't much liked by the other disciples, apart from John. The others were jealous that Jesus shared his knowledge with her and not them, and that she was his favourite. The last part of the quote, 'and the time will soon come when her tower shall stand alone by mine', seems to read that the role of the Magdalene will become known, and she will become as important as Jesus. When put together with the prophecy of Guillaume Béilbaste, he seems to infer that

Mary will stand beside Jesus and that time is now. Maybe we will see Mary in a different light, maybe her Rose line of Magdalene Priestesses will lead us out of patriarchy, into a new world where everyone is equal, treated the same, and love will be love, whoever we are.

The Gnostics

Until the discovery of the Nag Hammadi Gospels in 1945, the only references to the Gnostics were from Church writings. Gnostic comes from the Greek word, gnosis, which means to know, to have knowledge of God, an intimate deep knowledge without any priests or church necessary to intercede between the Gnostic and God. It is the self-knowledge, that comes from direct experience.

The Gnostics believe in an oral secret tradition directly from Jesus. The kingdom of God is within the Gnostics and they just needed to remain pure of heart, and remain responsible for their own soul, rather than relying on an eternal saviour or an institution. The goal is to free the soul from the material world. It is not an easy journey and not for the faint-hearted.

> Whoever has known himself, has at the same time already achieved knowledge about the depths of all things.
>
> The Book of Thomas the Contender

CHAPTER 4
RELIGIOUS TEXTS

Biblical Stories

The Bible in its original form is not the same Bible we have today. Mistranslations over the years have changed the meanings of several words.

The Bible was originally written in Aramaic, which was the language spoken around the time of Mary and Jesus. The texts were translated from Aramaic, into Hebrew, then into Greek, then Latin and medieval English, and eventually into modern English. With all these translations, misinterpretation is bound to happen – every translation changes the subtle meaning of the words.

The New Testament gospels of Matthew, Mark and Luke were written thirty-five to sixty-five years after the death of Jesus, with the first being Mark. According to the early Church historian, Eusebius, Mark worked very closely with Simon Peter, so the Gospel of Mark is possibly based on Simon Peter's accounts of his time spent with Jesus, as well as Mark's own memories. There is also the improbability of the stories being true. Do we really believe these things happened? Or are they myths, metaphors or mysteries? As regards mysteries, the word mysteria appears in the New Testament twenty-four times in conjunction with the teachings of Jesus.

> And behold, a woman in the city who was a sinner, when she knew that Jesus sat at the table in the Pharisee's house, brought an alabaster flask of fragrant oil, and stood at His feet behind Him weeping; and she began to wash His feet with her tears, and wiped them with the hair of her head; and she kissed His feet and anointed them with the fragrant oil.
>
> Luke 7: 37–38

The above quote is from the Gospel of Luke, and the assumption is that Mary Magdalene is the sinner referred to here, whereas in the Gospel of John, it is a similar scene, but it states it was Mary, the sister of Martha and Lazarus who bathed and anointed his feet.

Judaic Law at the time forbade women to uncover their hair in front of any man apart from her husband. Onlookers would have been shocked, as she appeared to have no regard for the law. In the Gospel of Luke, the horror shown was implicitly sexual and repentant, whilst in the Gospels of Matthew and Mark it focuses on the cost of the anointing nard. The washing of the feet and the anointing is a form of reverence, coming from a place of love. It was also against Judaic Law for a woman to publicly touch a man that she was not married to. Jesus rebukes other sinners but defends her actions – he refuses to condemn her. Why is this? Is it because he was in love with her? Was Mary Magdalene his wife?

> Now it came to pass, afterward, that He went through every city and village, preaching and bringing the glad tidings of the kingdom of God. And the twelve were with Him, and certain women who had been healed of evil spirits and infirmities – Mary called Magdalene, out of whom had come seven demons, and Joanna the wife of Chuza, Herod's steward, and Susanna, and many others who provided for Him from their substance.
>
> Luke 8: 1–3

In Christian eyes, Jesus is known as The Redeemer. The Bible states that Jesus cast out seven demons or evil spirits, depending on which version of the Bible you are reading, from Mary. He redeemed her and saved her, both from herself and for the sake of others.

In modern terms, what Jesus was said to have done for Mary could be viewed in many ways. Was this a chakra cleanse? Was it the removal of the seven deadly sins, vices or infirmities?

Could it have had something to do with seven levels of planetary ascension – sun, moon and five classical planets?

Classical planets were recorded by Greek astronomers in classical antiquity and are visible in the sky with the naked eye. From brightest to dimmest they are the Sun, the Moon, Venus, Jupiter, Mars, Mercury, and Saturn. Could it represent the descent of Inanna through seven gates going into the underworld?

Could Mary have partaken in a similar journey? Was Mary on a pathway to a symbolic initiation or rebirth? Could it have been an exorcism? If it was indeed an exorcism, that may explain why, apparently, during exorcisms carried out by a Christian exorcist, a Saint is said to sometimes show up to intercede between the influenced person and the demon. It is claimed that the Saint who most often shows up is St. Mary Magdalene – especially with sexual abuse victims or those who have been occult dabblers.

It should be noted though that it is questioned whether this really is Mary Magdalene, or some other entity using her name.

In the Gospel of Mary Magdalene, there are seven powers of wrath mentioned, and they seem to be describing an ascent of the soul. Seven is a number of completion, the holy spirit and eternity, and after the casting out process, Mary would have been seen as whole.

Whatever the removal of the seven demons was, Mary was a changed person afterwards. Before this, she was seen as a sinner and a penitent prostitute. Interestingly there is no mention of her being a prostitute in the New Testament or in any of the Gnostic texts. This is a more modern description and was possibly linked to the knowledge she would have gained from her temple training in sacred sexuality, and the views on this held by the patriarchal structure of the Church, and its suppression of the divine feminine. Pope Gregory, in 591 CE, talked about this episode of the seven demons being cast out of Mary in his homily 33 speech, delivered at the Basilica of St. Clement in Rome. He called her a sinful woman, and mentioned the Gospel of Luke and used that as justification for her being seen as unclean. He asserted that these demons filled her with loathing, hatred, and greed, that she was dirty, and that this was evidence that the anointing of Jesus and the use of perfumed oils, was a seduction attempt, as she lusted after him. Pope Gregory also confirmed that the woman who washed Jesus's feet with her hair and anointed him was Mary Magdalene, therefore the sinful woman,

Mary Magdalene and Mary of Bethany were one and the same.

By discrediting female sexuality in general, Pope Gregory was disempowering all women. It served the Church, both in Pope Gregory's time and Mary's time, to undermine Mary's teachings and her potential leadership role. As Mary was the first apostle, she should by rights have been the leader of the Church. This spread as gossip and became ingrained in people's minds. If the Pope says it, it must be true, right? This links into the darker side of her, the underworld aspect of her – she was cast out, unclean. Whereas in reality, she had power, the power of the strong feminine, and men feared this, and as a result, suppressed it. From this power came love,

Mary Magdalene has a large capacity to love and to spread the love, and this is the Mary we see described in the Gnostic texts. Notice that the above quote says, "The Twelve were with him, and certain women ... who provided for Him from their substance".

The Twelve referred to the male disciples, the women were not counted amongst these disciples, as though they were not good enough to be disciples in their own right, but Jesus and his group were happy to be funded by these women. The group of disciples was not unlike a gentleman's club where women were not allowed. The fact that the disciples were all men was also later used by the Vatican as a reason not to ordain women. Mary became one of Jesus's beloved followers, and being a woman of independent wealth, provided some of the money to financially support Jesus in his work. She travelled with Joanna, who was the wife of Chuza, Herod's steward, and his household manager.

Herod's palace would have been in Tiberius, which is a forty-five minute walk away. Mary was likely to have met Joanna at the court of Herod, so was she some kind of Courtesan? We know Mary was wealthy, so it was likely she socialised in these high-society circles. If, as the Church are happy to believe, Mary was indeed a prostitute, and it says in the Gospel of Luke that she was one of his financial supporters, it in turn means that Jesus and his disciples were happy to live off supposedly immoral earnings. According to the Catholic Church, Mary was not good enough to be a disciple, yet she could be a follower who provided the cash? How is this justified by the Church, I wonder?

> Now a certain man was sick, Lazarus of Bethany, the town of Mary and her sister Martha. It was that Mary who anointed the Lord with fragrant oil and wiped His feet with her hair, whose brother Lazarus was sick. Therefore the sisters sent to Him, saying,

"Lord, behold, he whom You love is sick." When Jesus heard that, He said, "This sickness is not unto death, but for the glory of God, that the Son of God may be glorified through it." Now Jesus loved Martha and her sister and Lazarus. So, when He heard that he was sick, He stayed two more days in the place where He was. Then after this He said to the disciples, "Let us go to Judea again." The disciples said to Him, "Rabbi, lately the Jews sought to stone You, and are You going there again?"

John 11: 1–8

So when Jesus came, He found that he had already been in the tomb four days. Now Bethany was near Jerusalem, about two miles away. And many of the Jews had joined the women around Martha and Mary, to comfort them concerning their brother. Then Martha, as soon as she heard that Jesus was coming, went and met Him, but Mary was sitting in the house. Now Martha said to Jesus, "Lord, if You had been here, my brother would not have died. But even now I know that whatever You ask of God, God will give You." Jesus said to her, "Your brother will rise again."

John 11: 17–23

Here we have confirmation that Mary the anointer and Mary from Bethany are one and the same. It is clear that Jesus and Mary cared about each other and that Jesus loved Mary's family too; 'Lord, behold, he whom You love is sick', and 'Now Jesus loved Martha and her sister and Lazarus'.

What if the death of Lazarus and his being brought back to life was a symbolic death only? An initiation rite of death through to rebirth.

I have even seen speculation that Lazarus is possibly John the Beloved who stayed at the cross with his sisters. There is uncertainty over the author of *The Gospel according to John*. Although widely accepted to have been written by St. John the Apostle, there are also some theories that due to the language and style of the writings, and the development of theology included in the writing, that this gospel may have been written at a later date, after John's death, and the author based the gospel on Johns teachings. It describes ministry in Judea and has a more mystical feel. John does not self-identify as the writer of the Gospel; the author refers to himself as 'the beloved disciple'. This is where the links to Lazarus start.

Lazarus is the only male person to have been individually emphasised as being loved by Jesus, he was called 'the beloved', or the 'beloved disciple'. Lazarus was not a travelling companion so it would explain why the text is more local-based. Interestingly, Lazarus was raised from the dead in John Chapter 11, and the first mentions of 'the beloved disciple' start in John Chapter 13.

Another possibility is that the story of Lazarus was written by another John at a later time. Over time, John and Lazarus have retrospectively been linked together and thought to be the same person. Due to 'the beloved disciple' being with Mary Magdalene at the cross, and no other disciples being present as they feared for their own safety, it has been believed that 'the beloved disciple' who was present was Lazarus supporting his sister and that he was there due to his love for his friend, Jesus. And so, the title of 'the beloved disciple' at the cross and in the Gospel of John have become linked over time.

Did Mary and Jesus get married at Cana?

> On the third day there was a wedding in Cana of Galilee, and the mother of Jesus was there. Now both Jesus and His disciples were invited to the wedding. And when they ran out of wine, the mother of Jesus said to Him, "They have no wine."
> Jesus said to her, "Woman, what does your concern have to do with Me? My hour has not yet come."
> His mother said to the servants, "Whatever He says to you, do it."

Now there were set there six waterpots of stone, according to the manner of purification of the Jews, containing twenty or thirty gallons apiece. Jesus said to them, "Fill the waterpots with water." And they filled them up to the brim. And He said to them, "Draw some out now, and take it to the master of the feast." And they took it. When the master of the feast had tasted the water that was made wine, and did not know where it came from (but the servants who had drawn the water knew), the master of the feast called the bridegroom. And he said to him, "Every man at the beginning sets out the good wine, and when the guests have well drunk, then the inferior. You have kept the good wine until now!"
This beginning of signs Jesus did in Cana of Galilee, and manifested His glory; and His disciples believed in Him.

John 2: 1–11

Jesus went to a wedding in Cana with his mother, his brothers and the disciples. It is where Jesus's first documented miracle took place. These events are not mentioned in any of the synoptic gospels – Matthew, Mark and Luke – only in the Gospel of John. When Jesus's mother told him that the wine had run out, he instructed servants to fill six large stone jars with water and Jesus turned the water into wine, a miracle of creation. But who were the bride and groom? We cannot be sure but there are some clues on who the happy couple could be. Mary, Jesus's mother seemed to be involved in the organisation as she seemed concerned and took responsibility for the wine running out. Why? Unless she was part of the wedding party, such as mother of the groom. According to Jewish custom, servants were only obliged to take orders from those in authority or the hosts. Also, traditionally in Jewish weddings at that time, the bridegroom poured the wine and served the guests. As well as priestesses anointing the future king and anointing the deceased prior to burial, brides anointed their grooms. Brides also washed their grooms feet. The anointing and feet washing were part of the marital rituals, the Jewish customs of that time. So, although there is no evidence of the marriage of Jesus and Mary, there is a possibility that the wedding of Cana was their marriage ceremony. If so, there is the presumption that Mary was there although she is not specifically mentioned, unless she is included with the disciples.

Magdala, where Mary is thought to have hailed from, is mentioned in the Miracle of the six loaves.

> Now Jesus called His disciples to Himself and said, "I have compassion on the multitude, because they have now continued with Me three days and have nothing to eat. And I do not want to send them away hungry, lest they faint on the way." Then His disciples said to Him, "Where could we get enough bread in the

wilderness to fill such a great multitude?" Jesus said to them, "How many loaves do you have?" And they said, "Seven, and a few little fish." So He commanded the multitude to sit down on the ground. And He took the seven loaves and the fish and gave thanks, broke them and gave them to His disciples; and the disciples gave to the multitude. So they all ate and were filled, and they took up seven large baskets full of the fragments that were left. Now those who ate were four thousand men, besides women and children. And He sent away the multitude, got into the boat, and came to the region of Magdala.

Matt. 15: 32–39

I have my own theory on this mass-feeding miracle. What if Jesus sharing out the few fishes and loaves had inspired others who had food with them to share it? That way a large quantity of people could have been fed, especially if it was market day and people were on their way home.

The number seven crops up here too. As we have already discussed, seven is the number of completion, as it is the day of rest in the creation story and also the number of demons cast out of Mary.

> There were also women looking on from afar, among whom were Mary Magdalene, Mary the mother of James the Less and of Joses, and Salome, who also followed Him and ministered to Him when He was in

Galilee, and many other women who came up with Him to Jerusalem.

Mark, 15: 40–41

Combining different versions of the bible, it appears to suggest that three Marys were present at the Crucifixion; Mary Magdalene, Mary mother of Jesus, and Mary of Clopas, who was thought to be his aunt, along with some other women followers, women who cared about Jesus and attended to his needs. But they were not given the title of disciples. None of the official disciples were present at the crucifixion, except John, the rest fearing for their own skin – although historical context is important here, in that the men were more likely to be arrested than the women.

Mary Magdalene anointed Jesus before his crucifixion, which was significant. This act sealed his role as King of The Jews. She remained with him throughout his death and cleaned and anointed him before burial, with the help of Joseph of Arimathea. This was also significant, as only family members were allowed to do this.

Mary's priesthood training would have covered funeral rites, so she would have been well-equipped for this important role. Handling corpses was not a very Jewish practice, as working with bodies or tombs was classed as unclean. This was a great indicator that Mary was either Egyptian or trained by the Priestesses of Isis in temples, as we know that the Egyptians were well practised with burial rites.

> But Mary stood outside by the tomb weeping, and as she wept she stooped down and looked into the tomb. And she saw two angels in white sitting, one at the head and the other at the feet, where the body of Jesus had lain. Then they said to her, "Woman, why are you weeping?" She said to them, "Because they have taken away my Lord, and I do not know where they have laid Him." Now when she had said this, she turned around and saw Jesus standing there, and did not know that it was Jesus. Jesus said to her, "Woman, why are you weeping? Whom are you seeking?"
> She, supposing Him to be the gardener, said to Him, "Sir, if You have carried Him away, tell me where You have laid Him, and I will take Him away."
> Jesus said to her, "Mary!" She turned and said to Him, "Rabboni!" (which is to say, Teacher) but go to My brethren and say to them, I am ascending to My Father and your Father, and to My God and your God.' Mary Magdalene came and told the disciples that she had seen the Lord, and that He had spoken these things to her.
>
> John 20: 11-18

> Now when He rose early on the first day of the week, He appeared first to Mary Magdalene, out of whom He had cast seven demons.
>
> Mark 16: 9

The term Rabboni is significant as it means teacher in Aramaic. It implies a student-teacher relationship. She left to tell the other disciples, casting her in the role of Apostle to the Apostles, although at this stage she was not recognised as such. This meant that she was chosen by Jesus to be the teacher of his word, his love, and his journey. The foundation of the Catholic Church, the Apostolic succession, is based on Simon Peter, St. Peter being the first disciple to see Jesus arise from the dead, even though the above quotes from the Gospel of John, and also the Gospel of Mark state it was actually Mary who saw him first. In fact, all four Gospels plus the actual Gospel of Peter place Mary at the tomb. It would appear that St. Peter was declared the first Pope and leader of the Church, because the Church wouldn't have a woman in this role.

There is a natural impulse to try to tie all the Marys together as a whole, but in doing that, we have to accept that Mary of Bethany, Mary Magdalene, and the foot washer are all the same person. The gap in years between the events occurring and the writing of the four

differing viewpoints of the Gospels, lead to this confusion. But the quotes above go some way to tying the stories and evidence together, demonstrating that they are likely the same person.

The Apocrypha – The Gnostic Gospels

The Apocrypha are the non-canonical texts which are not included in the modern Bible. The texts represent early Christianity, the teachings in their raw form, and supposedly how it was intended to be. The Gospels were written by a group of early Christians, who we would now call Gnostics, who were seeking a higher level of knowledge – the gnosis – thus the writings became known as the Gnostic Gospels.

These Gospels were written before Emperor Constantine changed the religion by controlling what went into the Bible, influencing the political and religious structure of the Roman Empire. The discovery of these texts had a revolutionary effect on the study of Christianity, turning some of the previously held ideas on their head, and enabling scholars to see the real relationship between Mary Magdalene and Jesus, and the friction between Mary and the disciples.

There are significant differences between the Gnostic Gospels and the Gospels in the New Testament. The New Testament canonical gospels chronicle where Jesus went, and who he met, with a bit of teaching and some parables thrown in. They were written from each of the disciple's viewpoints, and were recorded several decades after the events actually occurred. The Gnostic texts are more secretive, and mysterious, and teach us how to work on perfecting the human soul. Mary has a prominent role in the Gnostic texts but barely has a few mentions in the New Testament.

The Nag Hammadi Gospels

A lot of what we know about Mary Magdalene comes from a large set of documents found in the desert sands of Upper Egypt along the banks of the Nile, at a place called Nag Hammadi. These documents were found by two farmers digging sand at the foot of cliffs, near the river, in December 1945.

A stone jar of around half a metre in height, containing the Gospel of Thomas, The Secret Gospel of John, The Gospel of Philip, and The Gospel of Bartholomew, were found, amongst other important documents. Initially, the farmers were too scared to open the bottles fearing Djinn could be in there, but then the thought of treasure instead made them decide to smash the jars open. Unfortunately for them, but great news for academics, there were thirteen leather-bound volumes, known as codices which contained more than fifty texts.

It has been suggested that some of the Nag Hammadi Papyri may have been burnt as kindling by one of the farmers' mothers.

Was she unaware of the historical value? Or genuinely so poor she needed the heat from the ancient documents? It has been speculated that the family did in fact know the papyri value and sold them on to a dealer, inventing the kindling tale so that if questions were asked about missing documents they had a cover story. So, potentially there could be some undiscovered texts in a private collection somewhere.

With modern technology, the papyrus books have been dated back to the end of the 4th century and to the beginning of the 5th Century. They are likely to be copies of originals that date even further back in time. Some of these documents, the Gnostic scriptures, are currently in the Coptic Museum in Cairo, Egypt. In these Gospels, Mary is described as a teacher, a natural leader, and a source of great wisdom. The books give a more detailed picture of her importance and relationship with Jesus, and of her as the feminine aspect of Christ, the Magdalene.

Mary almost single-handedly evangelised the whole of France. She spoke of the true Christianity, the Rose Christianity. In the New Testament Gospels, Mary has a bit part, whereas in the Apocryphal Gospels, she is the star, the leading lady. Jesus refers to her in the books as 'The Woman who knows All', in the same way that the Goddess Isis was also known as 'The All'.

One theory is that the writings had been deliberately hidden and omitted from biblical records by Emperor Constantine, who declared himself a Pope and then set up the Council of Nicaea in 325 CE in an attempt to mislead the Roman Empire and hide the story of Mary and Jesus's true relationship. This council held meetings to vote on such things as dates, roles, and the administration of the Church as a whole. There were more than three hundred priests in the council, but any of these religious men who disagreed with Constantine were swiftly exiled. It was decided by a vote, that Jesus was a God, not a human prophet, so unifying the Roman empire towards Christianity.

This council of men was responsible for erasing the role of the sacred feminine, the real Mary Magdalene, from history. In 331 CE Constantine commissioned and financed the writing of a Bible, after confiscating any text, labelled heretical, that did not play into the 'Jesus is divine not human' narrative.

Incidentally, Emperor Constantine was a late convert to Christianity and was actually baptized on his deathbed, as he had continued to worship the Roman sun god Sol Invictus right up until his death. Constantine was actually a High Priest in this sun-worshipping Pagan cult.

Alternative theories of the Nag Hammadi Gospels include that the library was grave goods commissioned and deposited by Greco-Egyptian citizens, a process well documented in this region. It was thought that to be in possession of these documents around the 2nd century was actually illegal, as to practice Christianity was punishable by death, so they were hidden away. Another possibility is that the codices were hidden by a group of monks or a Gnostic sect, for safekeeping, away from the approaching Roman authorities.

The works were written in Coptic, a language containing both Ancient Egyptian and Ancient Greek words, between the 3rd and 5th centuries. The codices had likely been copied from original Greek texts which date as far back as the 1st century. The Gospel of Philip contains the Greek word koinonos, which has been mistranslated to mean companion. Its true translation should be consort or companion of a sexual nature – an intimate partner. This completely changes the meaning.

> And the companion of the [...] Mary Magdalene. [...] loved her more than all the disciples, and used to kiss her often on her mouth. The rest of the disciples [...]. They said to him "Why do you love her more than all of us?" The Saviour answered and said to them, "Why do I not love you like her? When a blind man and one who sees are both together in darkness, they are no different from one another. When the light comes,

then he who sees will see the light, and he who is blind will remain in darkness."

Gospel of Philip

The bracketed areas are missing or illegible in the original text. Here we see the true relationship between Jesus and Mary, which has been hidden and denied by the Church. Jesus sees something in Mary that the other apostles do not, he sees her as being superior to the other Apostles. Does the kissing on the lips mean they had an intimate relationship? The Nag Hammadi texts are symbolically written, so it could mean spreading the word of knowledge, and she was the only one who truly understood. There is another similar passage, also in the Gospel of Philip.

> There were three who always walked with the Lord; Mary, his mother, his sister and Magdalene, who was named his companion.
>
> Gospel of Philip

Here is the word companion again. Philip seems to imply in his gospel that they were sexual partners – husband and wife.

> Jesus said, "Whoever drinks from my mouth will become like me. I myself shall become that person and the hidden things will be revealed to that person."
>
> Gospel of Thomas

Drinking from the mouth means to listen on every word that Jesus says. Mary understood that words had power and were the main way that teachings were passed on. The Gospels of both Philip and Thomas mention a divine mother, a Sophia; a creatrix that is pure wisdom.

> Simon Peter said to him, "Let Mary leave us, for women are not worthy of life." Jesus said, "I myself shall lead her in order to make her male, so that she too may become a living spirit resembling you males. For every woman who will make herself male will enter the kingdom of heaven."
>
> Gospel of Thomas

This concerning quote shows that Simon Peter dislikes and does not trust Mary, but why does Jesus want to make her male? To have masculine strength? To be able to reach out and have disciples and followers of her own? Or could he be encouraging her to be empowered?

There is a Nag Hammadi Gnostic manuscript entitled The Thunder, Perfect Mind which talks about a divine feminine, a Goddess, revealing the following,

> For I am the first and the last. I am the honoured one and the scorned one. I am the whore and the saint. I am the wife and the virgin. I am the mother and the daughter. I am that one whose wedding is grand and has taken no husband. I am knowledge and

ignorance. I am strength and fear. I am stupid and wise. I have no God, and I am one whose God is great.

Below is a different translation of the same text. It shows how words can change the whole meaning of the text, and how they can be made to fit what you expect and want it to say. Notice the mention of Sophia in the second translation, but not the first one.

> I am the first and the last. I am the honoured one and the scorned one. I am the whore, and the holy one. I am the wife and the virgin. I am the mother and the daughter. I am called Sophia by the Greeks and Gnosis by the foreigners. I am the one whose image is great in Egypt and the one who has no image among the foreigners. I am she whose wedding is great, and I have not taken a husband. I am knowledge and ignorance. I am shameless; I am ashamed. I am strength, and I am fear. I am foolish, and I am wise. I am Godless, and I am one whose God is great.

This appears to have been quoted by a female. The text mentions Sophia, the divine wisdom, so potentially the words of Mary, especially with the Egyptian part of the poem. The words appear contradictory, equal but opposite to each other, reflecting the way that she is perceived by different people; those who respect and revere her and those who don't.

Supposedly, for a while, some of the previously discovered Nag Hammadi gospels were smuggled out of Egypt and landed in the library of Carl Jung, the Swiss Psychiatrist, who believed that the feminine aspect was buried deep within our subconsciousness.

The Dead Sea Scrolls
These scrolls are also known as the Qumran manuscripts. They were created in the years approximately 356 BCE to 50 CE and were discovered from November 1946 onwards, in Qumran, Palestine, on the northern shores of the Dead Sea.

The scrolls are both important and controversial and largely a mystery. They are thought to have been the library of a Jewish community called the Essenes. Ownership of the scrolls has been fought over by Arabs, Jews, and Palestinians. They contain secrets that have been lost over time and contain one of the earliest accounts of the Hebrew Bible. The scrolls were found by a goat herder on the west bank, alongside over 1,100 pieces of parchment and other materials, including pottery and ink. The Bedouins had been throwing rocks into the caves looking for a lost goat. They heard the sound of breaking pottery, and the first person who entered the cave found a series of ceramic jars containing animal skin parchments wrapped in linen.

They had possibly been hidden for protection, to stop the Romans getting at them. Some of the scrolls could not be unwrapped physically as they were charred, and some were falling into pieces. The goat herders informed the local archaeologists who, over the next ten years, discovered a total of around 850 scrolls across eleven different cave sites.

They were collected up and taken to Bethlehem, where initially they didn't realise the antiquity and academic value of the items and they ended up with the American School of Oriental Research in Jerusalem. It was only there, a year after their discovery that the importance of the scrolls was understood. John C. Trevor took some photographs and sent them to Professor W. F. Albright, a scholar, who responded that these scrolls were the most significant archaeological discovery of the 20th century.

It took many decades of research, but experts now tend to agree on who most likely created the library. The scrolls were created by a Jewish sect called the Essenes. An ancient elite group who demonstrably had a lot of knowledge across the Hellenistic world. They wrote down history to hand down through the generations and included astrology, horoscopes, the Essenes rules and lifestyle details. There were summaries of The Book of Genesis and parts of The Book of Enoch included. The scrolls revealed evidence of the development of religion in the times before Jesus's birth and during the times that he was alive. For forty years they were kept in secrecy by a monopoly of scholars, who happened to be all men, none of whom were Jewish, and they were not shared with worldwide experts. This was unusual for such a highly important set of documents. Clearly, they contained information that needed to be contained and kept secret. New additions have been filtering in for years from sites surrounding the Dead Sea.

Fragments then started to appear on the black market. The Wall Street Journal had four scrolls for sale in 1954. Since 2002 there have been approximately seventy fragments up for sale, some sold for millions, and about 90% of them are fraudulent copies. There have been many sales on the black market. The Museum of the Bible in Washington DC realised in 2020 that all the fragments they had were forgeries. Both Palestine and Jordan all lay claim to the scrolls but they are currently in the Israel museum. In 1991 Israel Antiquities opened up the scrolls to everyone digitally. The originals are currently being restored, and include several curses, protection spells against evil beings, and blessings.

Where do all these Gnostic texts fit in with Mary and Jesus's story? Mary is called the 'Woman who knows All' by Jesus in the Dialogue of The Saviour. In the text known as the Sophia of Jesus Christ, Mary tells Jesus that she feels intimidated by Peter due to his attitude towards females. Jesus reassures her that anyone divinely inspired by spirit can speak without fear, whatever their sex. It is clear in the apocryphal texts that Jesus considered Mary to be of high status, a natural leader, they had feelings for each other and that they were companions probably in a sexual way.

There are theories that Jesus escaped with Mary on the rudderless boat, and that he somehow escaped his crucifixion. This is a quote from one of the gospels, The Second Treatise of the Great Seth, the second tractate in Codex VII in the Nag Hammadi library.

> It was another, his father, who drank the bile and the vinegar; not I. I was beaten with a cane; it was another, Simon, who carried the cross on his shoulders. They placed the crown of thorns on another…and I was laughing at their ignorance.

This text is said to have been written from Jesus's perspective. The text is written clearly and is preserved in its entirety. So somebody could have been crucified in his place? If he had made it onto the cross, there were few spectators. He died rather quickly, even though crucifixion was meant to be a long slow death. What if the vinegar he was given was a drug, that made him comatose, faking death long enough for him to be put in the tomb?

A big speculation here is that it could have been a form of initiation, a near-death experience, a way for Jesus to commune with God. Could the Roman guards have been paid and in on the deception? Even pre-arranged with Pontius Pilate? He wakes up – a miracle, he has arisen. So he is whisked away quickly with Mary's group on the boat?

If this quote from the Nag Hammadi Gospels is taken at face value this could change the whole belief system the current Church is built on – that Jesus died to save us from our sins. No wonder these texts have been hidden away from public eyes for a long time.

The Gospel of Mary Magdalene
One of the copies of The Gospel of Mary Magdalene was not found at Nag Hammadi, it was actually found earlier, in Upper Egypt, along the river Nile and was sold to a German academic, Dr Carl Reinhardt in Cairo in 1896 at an antiquities market.

It was put into the Egyptian museum in Berlin and given its official title of Codex Berolinensis 8502, referred to as the Berlin Codex.

There were two other texts found with this Gospel, The Apocryphon of John and The Sophia of Jesus Christ, copies of which were also included in the

Nag Hammadi haul. It was written in Coptic, on ancient papyrus but was not in a well-preserved condition and was very fragmented. The first six pages were missing and it was only nineteen pages in length. Two other Greek copies have been found. Curiously, all three copies are missing the beginning, and four pages in the middle. Were these pages all destroyed intentionally? One of the 3rd-century Greek fragments is known as Papyrus Rylands 463 and was found at Oxyrhynchus in Egypt in 1917. The third copy, also in Greek was also found in Oxyrhynchus.

The Gospel explains Mary's struggles after the death of Jesus and her lack of acceptance by a group formed by the Apostle Peter, who struggled with female leadership. The other Apostles turned to Mary for reassurance and wanted to know the secrets shared with her by her Rabboni, Jesus. The text describes her as having visions and more superior knowledge than Peter.

The Gospel of Mary Magdalene was not written by Mary herself but by her students and the community around her, and was a way in for the feminine revival, as male dominance was becoming prevalent in the early days of Christianity. The Gospel shows that suffering and death are not the only way to enlightenment, and that spiritual development can come from mystical teachings. It is the only Gospel written in the name of a woman. This Gospel was a fifth-century copy of a document dating back to the second century.

As the first six pages are missing, the Gospel starts in the middle of a scene which takes place after the resurrection. Jesus talks about the nature of sin and the end of the material world. Jesus tells his disciples to go and spread his teachings but they are not happy, they have failed to understand the lesson given to them, except Mary who understood it.

When asked to explain why, she told the disciples about a vision she had when she communicated directly with Jesus. This made Andrew and Peter question why Jesus spoke to her and not them, and why such elevated teachings were given to a woman, suggesting that she is lying. Levi defends her when she starts to get upset, telling the other disciples to lay off her and go and do what Jesus requested, spread his teachings. Two things are unusual with this Gospel. The teachings are very much Mystery School-like, rather than direct preaching of the word. Teaching about the ascent of the soul, which appears to be an internal ascent, through the nous, through the levels of the ego. The other unusual thing about this Gospel is that the disciples are not happy to go out and preach, they are questioning the teachings, with Andrew even suggesting 'these teachings are strange ideas', as shown in the third Gospel and following excerpt.

> When the soul had brought the third power to nought, it went upward and saw the fourth power. It had seven forms. The first form is darkness; the second is desire; the third is ignorance; the fourth is the zeal for death; the fifth is the realm of the flesh; the sixth is the foolish wisdom of the flesh; the seventh is the wisdom of the wrathful person. These are the seven powers of wrath.
> Gospel of Mary Magdalene, Page 9

> Peter said to Mary, "Sister, we know that the Saviour loved you more than all other women. Tell us the words of the Saviour that you remember, the things which you know that we don't because we haven't heard them.Mary responded, "I will teach you about what is hidden from you." And she began to speak these words to them.
> Gospel of Mary Magdalene, Page 10

> Andrew responded, addressing the brothers and sisters, "Say what you will about the things she has said, but I do not believe that the Saviour said these things, for indeed these teachings are strange ideas."
> Gospel of Mary Magdalene, page 17

It has crossed my mind that these seven powers of wrath could be the seven demons that were cast out of Mary. The issue with this is that the events in Mary's Gospel take place after Jesus ascended, so a completely different time frame. She could be remembering the episode as she was describing a vision she had from the Saviour, of teachings that were just for her. But it seems too much of a coincidence for it not to be one and the same. The powers could have been classed as sins, as powers of the ego, as demons needing to be cast out.

After Mary described the vision she had, Simon Peter questioned her. This shows that he did not trust her, which is a theme running through the Gnostic texts.

> Peter answered and spoke concerning these same things. He questioned them about the Saviour: "Did He really speak privately with a woman and not openly to us? Are we to turn about and all listen to her? Did He prefer her to us?"
> Gospel of Mary Magdalene, Page 17

> Then Mary wept and said to Peter, My brother Peter, what do you think? Do you think that I have thought this up myself in my heart, or that I am lying about the Saviour? Levi answered and said to Peter, "Peter you have always been hot tempered. Now I see you contending against the woman like the adversaries.
> But if the Saviour made her worthy, who are you indeed to reject her? Surely the Saviour knows her very well."
>
> Gospel of Mary Magdalene, Page 18–19

Here, Mary is talking about a vision she had, a kind of ascent of the soul, or it could be an ascent within the heart, a form of personal transformation. Peter is questioning how she knows about this vision, and he complains.

The issue is not particularly with Mary but with women generally. Mary was trusted by Jesus, and this idea being reflected in the Gospels was not a good image for the Church, so that is why she was recast as a penitent, especially as sexuality was seen as the root of all evil, rather than as sacred and holy. A Church built on the foundations of a virgin mother and a celibate messiah was the goal, rather than the loving couple, Jesus and Mary. It is a form of control, and promotes an unrealistic lifestyle.

Peter appeared jealous of the knowledge shared with her by Jesus, he was not happy playing second fiddle to a woman. Peter was also known as Simon Peter. His birth name was Simon (Simeon) but Jesus changed his name to Peter (Petros) which means the rock. It appears that Jesus had planned for Mary to lead the Church, but

this was not to be. How different the Christian and Catholic Churches might be today if she had become the first leader.

So yes, it does appear that Jesus shared secret knowledge with her that he didn't want the other apostles to know. But here's something to think on, what if it was the other way around and Mary, as a sacred temple priestess, was the teacher of Jesus?

The Gospel of Jesus's Wife
Yes, such a parchment fragment does exist, but is it genuine or a forgery? This piece of ancient Egyptian parchment appeared in 2012 and was presented at a conference in Italy by Harvard Professor of Divinity Karen L. King. She is the author of *The Gospel of Mary of Magdala*.

The text is written in Coptic and the fragments contain the following phrases:

> Jesus said to them, 'My wife' …
> She will be my disciple.
> I dwell with her.

There are fourteen incomplete lines. We are assuming that Jesus had a wife but nowhere does it say Mary Magdalene.

We know that Jesus is unaccounted for, from the ages of twelve to thirty, so theoretically he could have had a wife, who he was no longer with, she could have died for example. He could be telling a story or giving some advice.

I would love it to be confirmation that he was in fact married to Mary, but sometimes if things appear to be too good to be true, they usually are.

Professor King thought the text was probably written in Greek a hundred years or so after the crucifixion, then translated into Coptic two centuries later. The fragment Professor King examined appeared to have been cut from inside the middle of another document and is about the size of a business card. It is owned anonymously and it does not have a clear provenance. The owner had purchased it along with five other papyri in 1999, from a collector.

The Vatican has said that it is a fake and it is likely to be a modern forgery on medieval papyrus.

Pistis Sophia
The Pistis Sophia is a Gnostic book dating to around 250-300CE, and was found in 1773, before the Nag Hammadi texts, and purchased by the British Museum in 1785. Pistis Sophia means Faith of Sophia or Faith Wisdom. Again, as in the pattern of Gnostic texts, it is based around mysteries and wisdom. It appears to have been written by two different people, an old man and a much younger person.

Twelve years after his ascension into heaven, Jesus returns to meet with some of his disciples to provide them with new teachings and ideas. He refers to wisdom as Sophia, and the goal of perfection. It's a difficult text to read, but it is clear to see the relationship between Jesus and Mary, and the loathing that Simon Peter had for her.

Mary, along with some of the other women, including Salome, do appear a bit like teacher's pets, and the first to answer the questions put forward by Jesus, so putting the other disciples' noses out of joint, which obviously doesn't go down well with the other male disciples.

Here is an example said by Peter in The Sixth Book, which is the last section of the Pistis Sophia,

> My Lord, let the women cease to question, in order that we may question.

The following phrase is repeated many times throughout the book,

> And Mary continueth again.

Good on you Mary for holding your own, as Peter gets more and more annoyed and says,

> My Lord, we will not endure this woman, for she taketh the opportunity from us and hath let none of us speak, but she discourseth many times.

Shockingly, Mary says this at another point in the text,

> But I am afraid of Peter, because he threatened me and hateth our sex.

It is important to remember here that Simon Peter, is St. Peter who was the first Pope and the earliest leader of the Christian Church.

It could be argued that these were roles that were stolen from Mary and it is very telling that the founder held misogynistic views, and used bullying tactics.

At one point in this text, Jesus says,

> Blessed Mary, you whom I shall complete with all the mysteries on high, speak openly, for you are one whose heart is set on Heaven's kingdom more than all your brothers.

The document ends with Jesus saying,

> Well done Mary, pure spiritual woman.

The Song of Songs
Also known as the *Song of Solomon*, or the *Canticle of Canticles*, this is an Old Testament book of erotic poetry, written by King Solomon, with the central character being the Queen of Sheba, the Queen of Ethiopia.

It has been associated with Mary, and possibly her sister Martha but we are not really sure why. Jesus is many times called the bridegroom (married to the Church maybe?) and linked with these poems. In doing so, we link Mary as the bride. It is similar to the stories of the Middle East, of Tammuz, Dumuzi and Adonis, where the goddess/bride goes to a tomb or garden to lament the death of their bridegroom and rejoices to find them resurrected.

The bride is wisdom incarnate, and the dove is symbolic. The Queen of Sheba was called Makeda or Magda in Ethiopia so there might just be a big hint right there, although she lived a thousand years before Mary. Could Magda / Magdalene be a title?

In some places, *The Song of Songs* matches ritual poetry written for Isis and Osiris word for word. Passages of the poems are read out in church on Mary Magdalene's feast day. It is explicitly sexual in nature, yet it is read out in the Catholic Church.

> How beautiful are your sandaled feet, princess!
> The curves of your thighs are like jewellery,
> the handiwork of a master.
> Your navel is a rounded bowl;
> it never lacks mixed wine.
> Your waist is a mound of wheat
> surrounded by lilies.
> Your breasts are like two fawns,
> twins of a gazelle.
>
> Song of Songs 7: 1–3

Here King Solomon is praising his new bride.

> Your mouth is like fine wine –
> flowing smoothly for my love,
> gliding past my lips and teeth!
> I belong to my love,
> and his desire is for me.
>
> Song of Songs 7: 9–10

The Queen of Sheba responds.

> Come, my love,
> let's go to the field;
> let's spend the night among the henna blossoms.
> Let's go early to the vineyards;
> let's see if the vine has budded,
> if the blossom has opened,
> if the pomegranates are in bloom.
>
> There I will give you my love.
> The mandrakes give off a fragrance,
> and at our doors is every delicacy –
> new as well as old.
> I have treasured them up for you, my love.
>
> Song of Songs 7: 11–13

Sexual encounter.

> Set me as a seal upon thine heart,
> as a seal upon thine arm;
> for love is strong as death;

jealousy is cruel as the grave;
the coals thereof are coals of fire,
which hath a most vehement flame.

Song of Songs 8: 6

This really does seem to be written about Mary and Jesus and the jealousy of Simon Peter, or at least links to Mary and Jesus can be made through the symbology.

A different story
The Akashic records of Thoth tell us that Mary gave birth to a son called John Martinus who was conceived after Jesus's resurrection with his light-formed body. Mary left the child in the care of Ionian priestesses on the Isle of Iona. *The Emerald Tablets of Thoth* are dubious at best and this theory has only been referred to for inclusivity.

CHAPTER 5
SYMBOLS RELATED TO MARY

The Nous

The Nous (pronounced new) is the eye of the heart and the soul. It's a Greek word that is difficult to translate. It is pure, an embodiment of great importance and a place to cultivate love. It is the intersection, an ascension from darkness to light, the portal between divinity and humanity, in our hearts but not in either the physical or the etheric. It is being acutely aware of and using all our senses. Between time and space, the nous is the wisdom in and of the heart, thinking with your heart, not your mind. A source of power from within us, the vision or perception of our soul. It is looking through your heart to meet the inner beloved, the divine source within each and every one of us, the purest part of our soul.

The first few pages of the Gospel of Mary are missing, and it is suspected that these pages told of how to activate this eye of the heart, how we work on developing it, and how we can step into the point of connection. Myrrophores would work with the nous, to balance the union between humans and the divine.[3]

---

[3] Myrrophores are temple priestesses trained in the sacred art of the holy oils which are used for anointing, healing, and burial rites.

Then Peter said to Mary, "Sister, we know that you are greatly loved by the Saviour, more than any other woman. Tell us those words of His that you remember, the things which you know and we don't, the teachings we never heard."

Mary answered, saying: "What is hidden from you I shall reveal to you. Whatever is unknown to you, and I remember, I will tell you."

And she began saying these words to them. She said, "Once I saw the Lord in a vision and I said to him: "Lord, [Rabboni,] now I see you in this vision.'

He answered me and said: 'Blessed are you Mary, for you do not waver at the sight of me. How wonderful you are! For this is where the treasure lies - in [that place where heaven and earth meet, where deep understanding arises in the heart and mind], 'the nous'."

I asked him this: 'Now tell me Lord, how does a person see such a vision, is it through the agency of their soul or through The Spirit?'

The Saviour answered: 'It is neither through the soul nor through The Spirit, but through the understanding which arises between the two, that is how the vision is seen.'

The Gospel of Mary Magdalene,
Page 10, thegospelofmary.org

The Vesica Piscis, Mandorla and the Yoni

A sacred geometry shape, the vesica piscis is made of two circles which overlap forming an almond shape in the centre. This central shape is known as the Mandorla (almond in Italian), and is also representative of the nous, the eye of the heart. It is a seed form for the flower of life's sacred geometry pattern, which can be seen in turn as the matrix for all the creations on Earth.

When the vesica piscis is vertical, the mandorla is the shape of an eye and the shape of the amygdala (Magdala?) part of the brain, it shows the union between soul and body, heaven and earth, above and below and represents the nous. Turning the vesica piscis horizontally, the mandorla forms a yoni shape; a birthing canal, a place of creation, a portal between the two circles, the holy of holies, one representing the male and the other the female linked together.

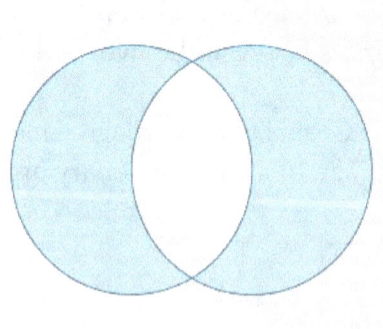
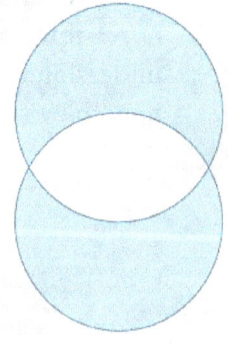

Vesica Piscis Horizontal　　　　　　Vesica Piscis Vertical

The vesica piscis is equal on both sides, representing balance and equality, true insight, and the bridge bringing together the opposites. The vesica piscis represents totality and oneness with existence when it appears inside a circle. Vesica piscis is Latin and it means 'bladder of fish.' Other names for the shape include 'the vessel' and 'the measure of fish'. The mandorla was known as 'the matrix' throughout the Hellenistic world, translated to 'the womb'.

In Christianity, the vesica piscis can symbolise the virgin birth, and that can also include the birth of a virgin universe, born from nothing, as well as a symbol of the holy trinity. The Christian fish symbol, the Ichthys, can be formed from the mandorla shape, and the mandorla also resembles praying hands. Three mandorla shapes together form the triquetra symbol, which is both a pagan symbol and Christian, in each case representing a trinity – in Paganism the realms of land, sea and sky, or the triple goddess for example. In Christianity, the father, son and the holy spirit.

The well head of the Chalice Well in Glastonbury is a vesica piscis pattern and there are also vesica piscis shaped pools in the Chalice Well gardens. The mandorla is featured in Christian art. Think of the architecture in churches and the paintings of Saints. It is used to form an enclosure or a halo, around the people in the painting. A good example of a painting showing the mandorla is Jesus and Mary Magdalene painted by Rosario con Meditazioni around 1308.

The vesica piscis and the central almond shape, the mandorla, are representative of the yoni. The Sheela Na Gig carvings on some Irish churches have prominent mandorla yonis representing the birth canal. Almonds are also a fertility symbol and were associated with the Goddess Cybele, her consort, Attis, and the nymph, Phyllis, who changed into an almond tree. The virgin nymph, Nana, conceived Attis by putting an almond into her breast, thus the almond has been linked with virgin births.

There is a trend amongst Magdalene priestesses to be womb healers, and creatrix, working with the cycle of birth, life, death and rebirth. Working with the power in our own holy grail spaces (our wombs), working with our sacred cycles and moon blood. Using the powers encoded within us to conceive ideas, heal, and awaken our scarlet womb space. They also work on ancestral matrilineal wound healing.

Some work with the white dove, the emerald heart and the red rose on the journey.

This all links in with Mary being the Goddess of sexuality. Obviously, there is more to this than I have gone into here. If you are interested in this type of work with Mary, check out the books in the recommended reading section. Also, portals, especially the Lionsgate 8/8 portal, light working and ascension codes have been linked with Mary too.

The Holy Grail

The first references to the holy grail were in the 12th century. During the Middle Ages the grail came to be regarded as a holy relic linked with Jesus. The holy grail is a chalice said to have been filled with the blood of Jesus from his crucifixion and collected by Joseph of Arimathea or Mary and taken with them to Glastonbury.

The term grail comes from the word graal, which originated from the word sangraal, which means royal blood. This has led to speculation that the chalice is symbolic of the womb of Mary, and that she carried the holy bloodline in the form of a holy child. The holy grail is a mystery and one of the most sought-after treasures, and is thought that it could have been the cup which Jesus and his disciples drank from at the Last Supper, or possibly the cup that was used to collect some of Jesus's blood at his crucifixion.

But is it a wooden or stone carved cup, a heavily adorned chalice, documents, or the holy bloodline? I have also seen the grail described as a table, a book, something fallen from the heavens, a depositary, and bizarrely, the severed head of John the Baptist on a platter. If indeed it is a cup, it is likely to have been made of wood and rotted away many years ago. Troubadours, who were bardic knights, moved around the courts of southern France and northern Italy during the 11th–13th centuries singing tales of courtly love, beauty of the natural earth, erotic poetry and stories of the holy grail, in Occitan, the language of the Cathars. As they travelled around, they were also accused of spreading heresy.

Wagner's Opera, *Parsifal*, is based on the 13th century grail story by Wolfram von Eschenbach. Using the story of a Knight who travels to an exotic country and falls in love with the Queen (could this be a veiled reference to Queen of Sheba?) it's a tribute to the bloodline of Mary and Jesus told through a Knight on a quest for the grail.

CHAPTER 6
THE ROLES OF THE MAGDALENE

Mary, the Priestess of Sacred Sexuality
The practice of womb wisdom is a way of working with holy energy in the womb centre. It is purification, a sexual healing of the self, a way of returning to our divine virginity. When the Gnostic texts talk about returning to our virginity, it means a return to our purity by reactivating and awakening the divine spark within us, ourselves, and our inner beloved.

Different energy centres in the female reproductive system vibrate at different energy frequencies, which we use to generate healing by sacred initiations, each one represented by a sacred rose. Our wombs take us from emotions of great pleasure, or great loss, from one extreme to another. We should celebrate this or work towards healing to feel bliss in the womb centre.

Mary likely trained as a qedesha, a priestess of sacred sexuality and tantric-like practices, and this may have been why Mary was twisted into having been a temple prostitute. This sacred sexuality does not exclude men, they can work on their divine phallic energy, reclaim their sexual power, the coming together in the bridal chamber of the divine feminine and divine masculine, or two other divine sexual energies, to join together spiritually as well as physically.

Mary the Myrrhophore, the Death Doula and Soul Midwife

The name myrrhophore comes from the Greek myrra, meaning myrrh and pherein, meaning to bear or to carry. Myrrhophores are women who work with the art of sacred oils. An ancient and secretive tradition that was started in the ancient Egyptian temples, centred around planetary alignments, and bodily illnesses, it was a celestial medical tradition, working on the physical, emotional and spiritual levels. These myrrh bearers took people through the mysteries of birth and death using holy oil. They were the death maidens; death doulas, holding the portal of death and rebirth open, they were psychopomps.

Death doula, or soul midwife work, would be used to guide souls through the transition from this world to the next. Mary possibly would have anointed Jesus with an oil before he went on the cross that would have acted as an analgesic, and maybe altered his consciousness too. She was his light, his guide and was trained to know the mysteries that went with each oil. There were nine sacred oils of Egypt that were used in a yearly cycle by the high priestess.

The nine oils were frankincense, sandalwood, myrrh, neroli, jasmine, ylang-ylang, lavender, blue lotus and rosa mystica.

The Pharaoh anointers were myrrhophores, and they could take you into a different state of consciousness with their exquisite knowledge of the oils, sometimes chosen by smelling your skin to see what oil you needed. They would work in groups of two or three, all working on your body at the same time, one working down the chakras and one working on the feet. The third used gemstones and made a sacred sound with them – now we use tuning forks and singing bowls. When they used the gemstones, they sang in unique tones so their voices, they could sense the unique sound of our body and replicate it. The teachings were mainly energy work which required understanding energy fields through instinct. Each energy centre was worked on separately, with specific holy oils for each, and the myrrhophore could sense what needed to be released. They learned about the nous, the wisdom of our heart and our soul, deep soul work, and our instinctive healing, with a dose of divine healing from the gods. It was a powerful but complicated holistic system. As well as being skilled in healing, they were trained to help people in the time before their death.

The Essenes also used holy oils for awakening the womb centre in a similar way to the myrrhophores. Womb work would have been used as a process of healing, releasing, rebirthing, removing and breaking ancestral lineage wounds.

They learnt a form of alchemy and worked by healing wounds from events in this life and in past lives, and they did this with the use of oils. It was a tradition that was passed down the female line, a sacred line, and myrrhophores were trained in a temple as soon as they reached puberty. Mary Magdalene is the most famous myrrhophore.

Mary the Shekinah
The Shekinah is a complex title, with many different definitions. Ask a dozen people and get a dozen different answers. The Shekinah has been translated from Hebrew as the 'dwelling place in the presence of God', the place one step away from God, where we aim to be. The term is not mentioned in the Bible but is in the Mishnah, Talmud, and Midrash Jewish texts.

The Talmud defines her as the manifestation of God, on Earth in a tangible form. In the Midrash, the Shekinah is defined as a separate female entity and the embodiment of wisdom, like the Greek Sophia. Jewish mystics saw her as the divine consort of God. But Shekinah has also been translated to be the female equivalent of a god, who sits at the side of God, and also as a dove, a sign for the presence of God.

The Gnostics think of the Shekinah as an exiled soul. Kabbalists see Shekinah as a female representing the Sophia, the wisdom of God, the breath of God but also in the shadow of God. She is a feminine Holy Spirit, a balance to the masculine God. She is essentially a feminine Jesus, who guides us from within.

The Israelites linked the Shekinah with the Cherubim, the fat-winged angel babies loved by the Victorians. Cherubim are described as an intermediary between God and mankind, so yes, it is easy to see why these pudgy angels have been likened to Shekinah. Mary is described as a Shekinah and is represented by the holy dove. Doves are sacred to goddesses of love including Aphrodite, Inanna/Ishtar, and Mary is also a goddess associated with love.

Mary the Egregore
As more and more people work with Mary, a thoughtform, an egregore, a magical entity, has been created by the collective minds. This archetypal energy has been named by the masses as Mary Magdalene.

Can this energy be directly worked with, and communicated with? It's as though Mary is being reborn through the awakened Rose Line, her priestesses, and from the collective wombs as we work to heal the matrilineal ancestral wounds we have been holding deep within us.

A new supportive sisterhood, a collective, every song, every note of music, every dance step, made by each of the devotees, the reawakened, works together, joins together to create this beautiful red harmonic – the sacred wisdom we can all tap into. It can strengthen us, we can put our own energy into the collective and when we need to, we can take energy from the collective. It will have energy imprints of other priestesses in it, so we can share and spread the love.

Mary the Goddess
Mary is a Roman Catholic saint, but I also believe she is a sacred feminine Sophia to Christ's Logos. I believe she embodies wisdom in the form of a goddess Sophia, a true power, and the duality of balance to the masculine energy of Jesus. She is a goddess of sacred sexuality and all things feminine.

I also see her as an ascended master, a human who has entered the higher spiritual realms of pure light, consciousness and pure awareness and is now an embodiment of a goddess. She can be seen as a mother of all creation and has knowledge and wisdom beyond

our imagination. A Shekinah in the presence of God. A beloved, holy one, independent of Jesus, a bride and mother. She is powerfully portrayed in the Gnostic texts, unlike the picture we get of her from the Church and the Bible.

She displays a triple aspect of mother, sister, and wife. She has been described as a dark goddess who is associated with the dark phase of the moon cycle due to her ability to heal, renew and regenerate. As a dark goddess she can help deeply ingrained negative patterns transform.

Mary was cast out and denigrated because she had power and men were afraid of this. She is a priestess trained in the practices of death rituals and as a soul midwife. She is a symbol of perseverance, she got through some of the worst trials a human being, a woman can go through. At the meeting in the Garden of Gethsemane, where she last saw Jesus before he was betrayed and crucified, they both talked and they knew that this was going to happen and that they would be tested to the limit. The torture and death of her loved one, in front of her, to which she had to bear witness and be strong, for Jesus as well as herself. Preparing his body for burial. Fleeing the country on a rudderless boat, being persecuted, and effectively becoming a refugee.

She did not have an easy life. She was cast as a whore, a sinner, a fallen woman, holding a powerful place in history. However, we can identify with her when we feel disrespected, unseen or even abused as women.

There has been a movement, a reclamation, a fight against the patriarchy, and the divine feminine is rising again. For two thousand years she has been cast into the underworld, but now she is reclaiming power. She seems to be a part of a larger archetype, a collective, an uprising of feminine consciousness on a worldwide scale. An embodiment of divinity but one that most women can resonate with. Almost a tool, a collection of ideas, an archetype, that we can work with in our collective and solitary practice. An energetic life force which we can tap into on a level unique to us. We are reclaiming the lost knowledge and the skills of the ancient priestesses. The Rose Women, of the secret paths who walked before us. Early Christianity was very different from the Christianity of today. The concept of sacred femininity was accepted in primitive Christianity, but this was later omitted from its belief system. It used to be a religion of compassion, but most of all, love.

Is she an impersonal cosmic energy? An independent spiritual being? A goddess? An aspect of ourselves? An incarnation of the Gnostic wisdom figure Sophia? Or all of these? How do you see Her?

Mary the Patron Saint
Mary is the Patron Saint of women, hairdressers, perfumeries, glove makers, tanners, pharmacists, penitent sinners, people leading a contemplative life, converts, people ridiculed for their piety, and last but by no means least, sexual temptation.

I notice that pharmacists are on this list. This is curious for me personally as I wanted to be a pharmacist, right back as far as I can remember in my childhood, while my friends wanted to be nurses or firemen when they grew up. How did I even know what a pharmacist was at that age? I even started training as a pharmacy technician but had to leave due to circumstances. I think, looking back, maybe Mary was making her presence known to me many years earlier than I realised.

In 1297 the Dominicans made St. Mary Magdalene their patron saint and the daughter, sister and mother of the order. The Dominicans were put in charge of the basilica with Mary's relics in but they were also the Order carrying out the Inquisitions, killing the Mary Magdalene-worshipping Cathars. The locals were not a happy bunch to say the least, especially being told they could still venerate her, but only on the Church's terms.

Is Mary a Sinner or a Whore?
Yes, she is but not for the reasons you would expect. First of all, there is no mention in the Bible of Mary being a prostitute. This idea was first presented by Pope Gregory the Great in 591 who preached about Mary's sexual sins.

In 1969 Pope Paul VI officially declared that she was not a prostitute and the readings made on her feast day changed to accept her as the first person to see the risen Christ, the apostle to the apostles.

How did she become known as a sinner and a whore?
In ancient times, a whore was a priestess of the Mysteries, especially in the cults of Isis and Inanna, and the Great Creation Mother was known as the Great Whore.[4]

The word Hierodulai, which meant sacred women, was translated from Greek, to medieval French and then into English as harlot.

---

[4] Information on this can be found in the Magdalene Mysteries by Seren Bertrand and Azra Bertrand.

In Germanic, Hores meant beloved ones. In Middle Eastern Semitic, Hor meant cave and womb. In Sumerian, Hur (pronounced Hor) meant sacred womb.

In Hebrew Horaa meant instruction, and Hor meant light. Horasis is an ancient Greek word for womb enlightenment, through sexual actions.

In the Bible, Horasis meant a prophetic vision. Harlot meant womb of light.

The title of Holy Whore was given to priestesses with an awakened womb. The word whoring is used in the Bible to tell of people who return to ancient goddess worship and consult Holy Whores.

Some ancient priestess titles from the Near East include: Hathors (Egypt), Harine (Babylon), Horae (Greece), Houri (Islamic Near East), and Harlot (Babylon/Canaan).

So as Mary was thought to have been an enlightened priestess of the mysteries, she was indeed a Holy Whore. For more on this theory, I highly recommend the book *Magdalene Mysteries* by Bertrand and Bertrand.

How is Mary a sinner?

Sin was an ancient Akkadian name for the moon and the name of the moon god/goddess, sometimes thought to be male, other times thought to be female. The moon goddess is at the centre of the womb mysteries. A sinner was a moon priestess who specialised in the womb mysteries of the monthly cycles of renewal and rebirth, so yes, as a priestess of Isis, Mary would have been trained in sacred femininity and sexuality and is therefore a sinner.

A gun salute to honour Mary Magdalene

Mary's Feast Day

Mary's Feast Day, is on July 22nd and is celebrated by the people of Provence as the day she came ashore near Marseille. Throughout Europe, many churches bearing her name light candles and incense in her honour on this day. The Song of Songs, written by King Solomon, is traditionally read on this day – here is the *I am the Rose of Sharon* reading, which is an example of one of the readings used.

> I am the rose of Sharon, and the lily of the valleys.
> As the lily among thorns, so is my love among the daughters.

> My beloved is mine, and I am his:
> he feedeth among the lilies.

Even to this day, her skull is taken on a procession through Saint-Maxime-la-Sainte-Baume and many pilgrims attend this celebration and the nearby grotto of Sainte-Baume. In 1969 the Church in Rome cleared her of being a prostitute, finally, by saying that Mary Magdalene, Mary of Bethany, and the sinner in the Gospel of Luke were not in fact the same person. This is in conflict with some of the evidence in Bible quotations that say that she is, in fact, the same person. But I am just relieved that the Church has now accepted Mary and cleared her name.

In 2016, on her feast day, the Church finally officially declared her the Apostle of Apostles, as she was the first to see the risen Christ and spread the word to the other disciples. This announcement upgraded her Memorial Day to a Feast Day and now is an official celebration within the Catholic Church. This puts her on the same level as the other apostles, with all the liturgy on that day being specifically oriented towards her. Great news but it took until 2016 for this change to happen and there was no big announcement. Most people didn't get the memo and still refer to her as the penitent prostitute.

CHAPTER 7
SACRED SYMBOLS, FLOWERS AND EPITHETS

Mary's Sacred Symbols

Alabaster jars are the symbol most commonly associated with Mary. She carried a jar containing spikenard (nard) oil ready for anointing her king, her teacher, and her lover. The oil was very costly and so were the alabaster jars.

The jar represents our body as a vessel – a container for our soul. The jar can symbolize the light, our divine light within us, the love contained inside. Nard is a very strong, concentrated oil steamed from the rhizomes (tuberous roots) of the spikenard plant and its botanical name is nardostachys jatamansi. Nowadays it is generally found in Nepal, Israel, and India, but in Mary's time it was thought to only have been available from Nepal, so as well as being costly, Mary would have needed to have known someone who travelled the trade roads all the way from Nepal. Joseph of Arimathea was a merchant, so he was possibly her supplier.

It's a different nard now to what would have been on the market then; the oil we have now is amber-coloured as opposed to the green heart centre-coloured oil Mary would have worked with, and it now smells a little like patchouli. It was and still is expensive – 10ml runs at about £50. Patchouli oil is a good substitute to use. Mary had a great deal of wealth, due to her noble birth and this is one of the reasons she was readily accepted by Jesus's disciples and followers, as she funded their lifestyle and work along with several other wealthy women. Being a priestess and healer, she knew her role was to anoint and make, Jesus the King of the Jews, the Messiah. The Hebrew word Messiah means the anointed one.

Skulls have been depicted in paintings such as *The Penitent Magdalene*, by Titian, *The Repentant Mary Magdalene* by Domenico Feti and *Magdalene with the Smoking Flame* by Georges De La Tour. The skull is said to remind us of our own mortality and that as one day we will die, we should devote our hearts to God. Mary is shown in contemplation with a skull, knowing her death is approaching before immersing herself in prayer. Mary stares at the skulls reminiscing of her lost love.

An outlandish theory I have read could link to this symbolism in the paintings, that Mary was the custodian of the head (skull) of John the Baptist. She took it with her when she fled Israel and somewhere along the line it ended up as either worshipped by the

Knights Templar, or the secretive treasure that was being squirreled away by the Cathars. Incidentally the Cathars hated John, whereas the Knights Templar loved him. Both groups were thought to have done magical work with or drunk from the skull. Some theorists suggest that this head / skull on a platter is actually the holy grail. Interestingly these paintings also depict the next symbol, the book.

Open books are sacred to Mary Magdalene, as she is the source of wisdom, the Sophia, the guardian of the mysteries imparted to her by Jesus. Representative of the hidden Gospel of Mary Magdalene, the book is the place of secrets, the embodiments of wisdom, and hidden knowledge. Mary spread the word of early Christianity, as it should be, rather than the heavily culled version and multiple translations with changed words that we have today.

A chalice is a sacred symbol for the Magdalene, which could represent the female sexual organs as Mary is associated with divine sexuality, and it could also allude to the possibility of a sacred bloodline. It could also mean holy water, as goddess or saint shrines are regularly near springs, wells, or other water sources. It is a cup, a vessel, a symbol of the feminine, fertile, the goddess, the power of the divine, the bringer of life. A chalice is a common symbol representing the waters of life, and the flowing of knowledge, it is a receptacle, containing secrets that are yet unknown.

A symbol of mastery, the cup represents receptive feminine energy, the bulging belly of a pregnant woman, whereas the stem of the chalice presents the masculine on its journey up towards ascension. The base of the chalice represents grounding as wisdom from the heavens is poured down into it. All parts together bring about balance and form a vessel of light energy. The holy grail could be a chalice that makes you immortal if you drink from it, the cup that collected the blood of Christ at his crucifixion, the womb of Mary, a series of holy documents, or the holy bloodline from the Magdalene.

Mirrors feature in some of the paintings of Mary, she is seen sitting in front of them. Mary is seeing through the eyes of her soul. An inscription from the Temple of Apollo in Delphi is apt here – know thyself. That's what mirrors encourage us to do, and this is an important part of the modern work of the Magdalene priestesses.

The Penitent Magdalene

Mirrors are a symbol of vanity, they reflect the world back at us and encourage us to look deep within, to what we see in our heart, and beyond what we see reflected back at us. Candles in the paintings reference her spiritual enlightenment, with the burning down of the candle representing the fragility of life, that may extinguish at any moment.

Grapevines are said to depict the holy bloodline and are where the name Merovingian (Mer, Mary and Vin, Vine) comes from. The Merovingians were a line of French kings who were said to have descended from the Mary and Jesus bloodline and are protected by The Priory of Sion, if such an organisation does in fact exist. In my personal practice, I use bramble vines, which I use to represent balance of equality; opposites coexisting with each other, the thorns and the fruit.

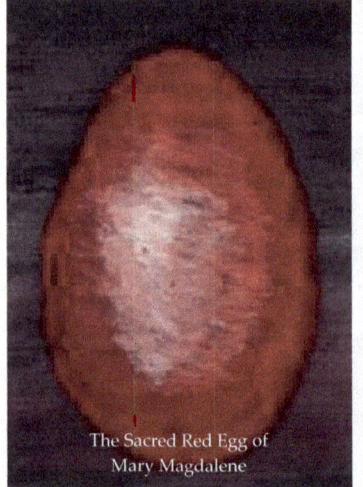
The Sacred Red Egg of Mary Magdalene

A red egg is sacred to Mary. Orthodox Christian legend tells of a story that Mary told the dinner guests of Emperor Tiberius Caesar on a visit to Italy, the story of Jesus's resurrection.

Caesar ridiculed her, and said that a man could no more rise from the dead than the egg in her hand turn red, and with this the egg immediately turned red. An alternative legend says that rather than Mary recounting the story of Jesus's resurrection, Mary actually confronted Tiberius Caesar over the role that Pontius Pilate played in getting Jesus arrested. These legends are likely to play a part in the role of painted eggs at Easter time as well as the resurrection stories and fertility cycle of the land. The red eggs form an important part of the Orthodox Christian celebration of Pasha, which we celebrate as Easter.

Venus and the rose formation is a phenomenon linked to Mary Magdalene. Venus has a 225-day year, so to form the pattern of the five-petalled rose, which is also a pentagram, from the perspective of the earth, it takes an eight-year cycle to complete it. Venus has five rotations each of nineteen months, which each forming a petal. The last Venus rotation started a new eight-year cycle in June 2020.

Rose of Venus

With cyclical qualities, the pattern formation displays beauty and perfection, and this formation has been tracked for thousands of years and is known as the rose journey of Venus. The rose buds, blossoms then dies, and then is reborn again. The five petals can be representative of the feminine pathway through life, birth, menstruation, becoming a mother, menopause and then death. The Rosa Rugosa species of rose, along with some other wild roses have five petals. As we already know, the rose is a sacred symbol of Mary Magdalene.

The Camargue Cross, also known as La Croix de Camargue and the Guardians Cross, is the symbol of the French region of Camargue, of which Saintes-Maries-de-la-Mer is the capital. It is a beautiful region known for its white horses, and pink flamingos.

The Camargue cross is made up of lots of threes. There are three symbols, an anchor, a heart and a Latin cross (a Latin cross is the classic Christian cross). The top part of the cross also represents a trident, a three-pronged fork, and a working tool. The Camargue cross represents three virtues, with the cross representing faith, the anchor hope and the heart is for charity and love, and the three Marys who arrived on the shores of the Camargue. So the cross represents faith, hope and love.

> *"And now abide faith, hope, love, these three; but the greatest of these is love."*
>
> 1 Corinthians 13: 13

The symbol is found on display throughout the region and was designed by the artist Hermann Paul in 1924.

The Star of David, the six-pointed star of the Jewish faith, links Mary and Jesus together. It is made up of two triangles, one pointing up and one pointing down. On one level it represents the blade and the chalice coming together. The triangle pointing up represents the phallus, the blade, and the triangle pointing down represents the womb, the chalice. The fire and water symbols are in perfect union, and equal sizes, representing the balance of male and female. A sign of sacred union and marriage. On another level, it represents 'as above, so below', the heavens and the earth and the balance between the two, the relationship between man on earth and God in the heavens.

Red is the colour of the divine feminine, sacred sexuality and holy bloodlines. It is the colour of vitality, of transformation. Red is the colour of our heart and blood, of blood wisdom, an essential part of our being. The red thread that connects us all together, regardless of gender, red is love, and love is equal. Love is why we are all here, our purpose. To love each other, love the world, but the true source of love is from within. Mary can help us see this love, and to develop this as we learn to love ourselves. Mary is the connection between the source and ourselves, between the love and our souls. But red also represents sexual sin, physical passion and the pure, raw pain of sufferance and is the symbolic colour of the womb priestesses. The Reddening is also a spiritual alchemical stage where the lowest form and the highest form join together, and this is one of the purposes of the divine energy of the Magdalene, joining together with the Christos energy.

Doves are a symbol of the sacred Magdalene. Magdala overlooks the Valley of the Doves on the western shore of the Sea of Galilee. Magdala can be translated as the dove within the place of doves, and they were bred here at this sacred place. These birds are sacred to Venus and represent the Holy Sophia. A guiding symbol of light, doves represent alchemy and divination, and are well known as a symbol of Christianity. Doves, as well as a symbol of peace, are linked with Aphrodite and are representative also of sexual passion, lust, sexual union, and the yoni.[5] As regards to divination, in the Hebrew Kabbalah, Jewish and Greek practices, it is known as ornithomancy, the practice of reading the omens from the behaviour of birds, counting them, listening to them etc.

---

[5] https://symbolreader.net/2014/06/07/the-symbolism-of-the-dove/

In the Song of Songs, the bridegroom refers to his beloved as the dove. The dove is an emblem of the Shekinah also, linked with the healing presence of the divine mother and daughter. When Jesus was baptised by John, a dove appeared.

> When He had been baptized, Jesus came up immediately from the water; and behold, the heavens were opened to Him, and He saw the Spirit of God descending like a dove and alighting upon Him. And suddenly a voice came from heaven, saying, "This is My beloved Son, in whom I am well pleased."
>
> Matt. 3: 16–17

My guess would be that the goddess descended during this ritual, rather than the god, who spoke from the comfort of the heavens. The duality of male and female in practice.

> Behold, I send you out as sheep in the midst of wolves. Therefore be wise as serpents and harmless as doves.
>
> Matt. 10: 16

This quote is Jesus talking to his disciples. The Bible sees the dove as representing purity.

Cinquefoils (French for five leaves) are five-petaled decorative stone rose flowers, usually decorating the tops of stone gothic arches, mostly but not always, in churches from the Middle Ages. They represent maternal love and are associated with the womb of Mary. The Romans called this symbol the Rose of Venus, representing womanhood and natural beauty. Often seen as a rose stone-formed window. The cinquefoil flower is potentilla, which is a member of the rose family, so a five-petalled rose.

In the Bahá'í faith, Mary is seen as the 'Lioness of God', a courageous woman, a role model in a hostile environment, determined in her mission to spread the word of God. She is very highly respected. But here there is the divine alchemy of the dove and the Shekinah, contrasting with the ferocious lioness, they are opposite states.[6]

Sacred flowers
The Rose of Sharon. Said to have been quoted by the Bride of Christ, the rose of Sharon could be a mistranslation and mean crocus, white daisy or some other flower that grows in a field instead. Rose of Sharon is not known to grow in the area of the Sea of Galilee. Further research leads me to believe that the rose of Sharon could possibly be the cistus plant, which now

---

[6] Mary Magdalene: Lioness of God in the Bahá'í Faith
https://bahai-library.com/osborn_mary_magdalene/

grows in the Languedoc region. Cistus plants help balance duality, especially of ego and spirit.

"I am the rose of Sharon, and the lily of the valleys".
Song of Solomon 2, chapter 2:1

Lily of the Valley is also known as Our Lady's Tears, symbolic of the tears shed at the Crucifixion. Sacred to the Virgin Mary, Jesus's mother who was present at the crucifixion too.

The rose is a symbol of secrecy and silence and was often hung from ceilings as a reminder of discretion about discussions taking place. This was an ancient Roman custom, known as sub rosa, under the rose.

The rose means purity, transmutation, and joy, it is also a symbol of sexuality, the womb of the goddess, especially the rosebud, is ripe for being opened. Alchemically the rose represents wisdom. One of the highest frequency flowers, its extracts help our spirit to awaken and open up our heart centre. The red rose of sexuality is a symbol of Mary Magdalene, and the white rose of the pure, virgin mother Mary. See the contrasts between the imagery of the two Marys here?

The red and the white roses together suggest completion, of the cycle of death and renewal. The centre is hidden, representing secrecy, whereas the whole flower shows plenitude. The blossoming rose is a representation of female external genitalia, of sensuality and seduction. Thorns represent pain and blood, think of the crown of thorns, and the symbolism of the blood of Christ being spilled whilst on the cross. The rose is also sacred to Venus, and roses can raise spiritual frequencies. The word rose is identical in English, French and German, and is an anagram of Eros, the Greek God of sexual love. In Rome, the rose was known as the flower of Venus and the emblem of the sacred prostitutes.

The lily is representative of the Fleur-de-lis, which symbolises the French royal blood lineage of the Merovingian theory and is also a symbol of the Holy Trinity. It has foliage shaped like blades, representing a heart pierced by sorrow. Fleur-de-lis also represent the northern point on a compass, which is also known as a compass rose. I like to see this as Mary subconsciously guiding us through our lives.

The marigold comes from the words Mary's Gold. It is a species of calendula that grew around the Dead Sea and hills in Galilee and was macerated in olive oil and used to heal wounds and prevent infections. As Mary used anointing oil in the New Testament, this plant has become sacred to her. It helps with vulnerabilities and adjusting to changes. The particular species that Mary would have used in Israel, appears naturally in one place in Europe, the Languedoc region in southern France, how synchronous is that?

The orange blossom is a symbol of purity. Mary is holding an orange blossom flower in the painting of *Martha and Mary Magdalene* by Caravaggio dated 1598, Mary's other hand is on a mirror. The orange blossom is traditionally used as a flavouring in navette cakes.[7]

The mayweed (matricaria inodora), which is sacred to Athena has become associated with Mary and is known as St. Mary's herb.

Mary's Epithets

What is an epithet? An epithet is an attribute or characteristic given to a person, in this case the divine feminine Mary. It is a descriptive word, a way of describing personality traits, a means of identification or behavioural patterns for example. Here are some of Mary's epithets:

---

[7] The navette cake is a cylindrical sweet-pastry from Marseilles baked in the shape of a boat (navette); a 7–8 cm long oval with the ends tapered in sharply. It commemorate the arrival of St Lazarus, Mary Magdalene and Saint Martha at Saintes-Maries-de-la-Mer.

The Chalice.
The Holy Grail.
The Holy Vessel.
The Rose.
The Divine Mother.
The King Maker.
Our Lady of Witness.
The Divine Mary.
Rose of Sharon.
The Queen of Love.
Sangraal.
Watchtower.
Great Tower of Strength.
Cosmic Doorway.
Matriarch of the Vine.

Mother of Love.
Magdalena.
Keeper of Doves.
Mystical Rose.
Black Madonna.
Apostle of Apostles.
Woman with Alabaster Jar.
Myrrh Bearer.
Ain Soph Aur (limitless light).
Opener of Ways.
Priestess of the Inner Fire.
The First Pope.
Goddess Sophia.

Spirit of Sophie, she of overwhelming, undeniable wisdom.

Maryam, Miriam, Maria, Miraye, Maga, Maj, Magi, Maraye – all Priestess titles.

Mary Lucifera – Mary the Light Bringer – she was given this title in France whilst she was establishing her teachings there.

Goddess Diana Lucifera was worshipped in the same area where Mary lived, so there may have been some conflation between the two. Mary is said to have brought the holy light and holy fire and has been called an 'illuminatrix', the bestower of enlightenment. The Gnostics used the title Mary Lucifera for her, seeing it as a great honour and reverence.

Mary Gardens
A Mary Garden is a garden dedicated to Mary Magdalene, Mother Mary and Jesus with statues and shrines alongside benches dedicated to them. Popular in monasteries and convents, it contains sacred plants, as well as others planted for their attributes such as Forget-me-Nots, or Mary's Rose (Peony). Planting schemes are available such as 'walk the rosary'. Gardens should be enclosed if possible, a hortus conclusus, based on the fourth chapter of Solomon's Canticle of Canticles:

> A garden enclosed
> Is my sister, my spouse,
> A spring shut up,
> A fountain sealed.
> Your plants are an orchard of pomegranates
> With pleasant fruits,
> Fragrant henna with spikenard,
> Spikenard and saffron,
> Calamus and cinnamon,
> With all trees of frankincense,
> Myrrh and aloes,
> With all the chief spices –
> A fountain of gardens,
> A well of living waters,
> And streams from Lebanon.

The Persian word paradise means an enclosed garden. The gardens are a place of solitude, remembrance, and a great place for meditation practice or lighting a votive candle. The time spent designing and maintaining the garden is part of the devotional process, and has been likened to a form of zen garden.

There is a Mary's Garden project running in Philadelphia that was founded in 1951 which researches flowers identified with Mary Magdalene, the Virgin Mary and Jesus, and provides seeds. A small potted version can be made and placed on an altar.

CHAPTER 8
MARY, THE DIVINE FEMININE

Matriarchy versus Patriarchy

When working with the divine feminine energies of Mary it is easy to forget the partnership she had with Jesus. We all have feminine and masculine qualities within us, and it can be hard for us to keep them in the correct balance.

Times are changing and there appear to be antipatriarchy sentiments growing and dynamics are changing. But is it helpful? And for whom?

If we think of a pendulum with patriarchy on one side and matriarchy on the other, there has been a shift from the Goddess-worshipping cults of antiquity, right over to the patriarchy of the modern Catholic Church, completely swinging through the middle ground. It would appear that some feminist groups are trying to swing the pendulum right over to the other side again, but what if we can get it to stop in the middle? A place of equality and balance?

Patriarchy and matriarchy are very different from each other. What did the men think of the Goddess-worshipping matriarchal cultures? Could it have been a time of mothering or smothering? What if the men had fought hard for control and pushed the pendulum right across? Even the cross is a visual sign of the imbalance within Christianity. The vertical bar which represents the masculine is longer than the shorter horizontal feminine bar, which in itself makes it an appropriate symbol for suffering. What impact is the 'Hex the Patriarchy' campaign having on men?

In the main Abrahamic religions, God is referred to as 'Father', ensuring that the divine is seen as masculine; what effect is that having on women?

Maybe we need to listen to a new dialogue, one that balances our spirituality within ourselves. Find a way to harmonise.

The Church stripped the feminine teachings away; they were the true spiritual teachings, the Apocrypha. There were teachings of balance within humanity, a different way of interpreting the messages from God. If one side is suppressed it is likely to erupt – an antagonistic route on the path of destruction, just like Kali. We as a collective need to bring the feminine back into the Church's teachings, the Rose Christianity, and the path of the Magdalene, but working alongside the divine masculine Christos energy, and bringing them together in balance.

Goddess Sophia

The Gnostic Goddess, who is equated with Mary, is known as the sacred light, 'the all'. She is also associated with the Goddess Isis. She is the expansive, everlasting light, of this world and the world beyond, both of spirit and of matter, from the place that precedes birth, the gestation of life, of pure potential, and she transforms spirit into matter.

CHAPTER 9
MARY IN THE ARTS AND MEDIA

Mary's Appearance in Art

The Mary Magdalene depicted in art tended to have golden red hair flowing wildly, pale skin, and she was portrayed in various states of undress, provocatively, in red clothing, or sometimes naked – a scarlet woman.

Mary was sexually empowered through her training within the Cults of Isis. She was independently wealthy, not under the control of a male, be it father, husband, or son – she did not need to sell her body. The Church cast her as a prostitute and destroyed early apocryphal texts which showed her as a strong, clever woman who was important to Jesus. In art she was depicted as sad, moping, and gazing as if in some form of torment or penitence. Fair of face, blackened name, what a whitewash.

Contrast this to the Church's description of the Virgin Mary. Virginal and chaste, submissive, one dimensional, insipid, and powerless, and always depicted fully clothed. This is how the Church wants women to be portrayed – it suits the Church's patriarchal narrative.

Given the region that Mary was born and lived in, it is much more likely that she did not have long flowing red hair but was in fact dark dark-haired and olive-skinned but those depictions of her are rare. I have read that it is possible that the Tribe of Benjamin, which Mary was born into, was known for having ginger hair and fair faces, but we cannot be sure of this fact. I have also read that a few ginger hairs were found on Mary's skull, although there are theories that she may have been born in Egypt, or even Ethiopia so may actually have been dark-skinned. Could the fact that Mary was depicted as light-skinned and fair-haired, be a case of how beauty was defined at each time in history? Or could there be a level of whitewashing going on?

The church are known to depict Jesus with blonde hair, pale skin and blue eyes, and Mary Magdalene has not avoided these image stereotypes either. In most images of her, she is shown with pale skin, fair ginger hair and is usually in a solemn, despairing repose or with a sinful look in her eyes. Stained glass windows and church paintings show her this way, either subconsciously or consciously portraying her with lighter skin tones than she is likely to have had, given where she was born and the region she grew up in. These pale, European-style images can be found in paintings and artworks throughout the ages.

Hidden symbols and links to Mary can be found in many artworks. In her book, *The Woman with the Alabaster Jar*, Margaret Starbird discusses a secret language made up of emblems that was used by heretical Christians in late medieval Europe. These Christians believed that Mary and Jesus were married and that there was a royal bloodline carried by their descendants, and they concealed emblems representing this in artwork and included symbols such as mermaids, unicorns, towers, castles and the Fleur de Lis.

In a few altarpieces produced in the Middle Ages, showing her either at the entombment of Jesus, or with the twelve apostles, she is presented as taller than them, showing her significance. Others show her being assumed to heaven, like the virgin mother was, showing her divinity. These depictions are in museums and remote churches throughout Germany and France. There is a mural painting of Mary Magdalene in St. Patrick's chapel in Glastonbury Abbey, which is said to represent the driving out of the seven demons from her, it depicts six dragons coming out of her with the seventh deadly sin being her, as prideful.

The Ghent altarpiece, *The Adoration of the Mystic Lamb* painted by Hubert and Jan van Eyck in 1432, is worthy of a whole book on its own. It is painted in oil on wood and is installed in St. Bavo's Cathedral in Ghent,

Belgium. With foldable wings, it measures 3.4m x 4.6m when fully open. There is hidden symbology in the painting, just like Da Vinci's *Last Supper*. For a good in-depth analysis of this painting, I recommend reading *Magdalene Mysteries* by Bertrand and Bertrand.

Catholic icon art are religious images for devotion and prayer. The word icon comes from the Greek word eikon, which means image. Generally, the saints are painted on wooden panels, with a halo and possibly some gold leaf.

Hairy Mary
Hairy Mary images present Mary as being covered top to toe in hair, unkempt, wild, more like a banshee than a beautiful woman.

There are various paintings, such as *St. Mary Magdalene* by Giovanni Pietro Birago, painted in the 15th Century, that appear to depict Mary covered head to toe in hair, appearing like a female Wookiee. She is shown being ascended into heaven carried by angels (the Assumption).

The story is that Mary went into the desert, as penance and to pray. Whilst there she became so focused on the penitent prayer that she neglected herself and her clothes became rags. In order to protect her modesty, the Almighty decided to cover her up by sprouting hair all over her body giving her the appearance of a Wookiee. Or it could just be that her hair grew very long as she had no means to cut it, so it covered her naked body.

The problem with this story is that there are also tales of a Saint Mary of Egypt who died in the fourth, fifth or sixth century, depending on which account you are reading. She was not allowed into the Holy Sepulchre in Jerusalem and she fled to the desert to live as an ascetic hermit, having spent much of her life after the age of 12 as a harlot giving out freebies to sailors. Whilst in the desert she was said to have survived on just three loaves of bread and any herbs she could find in the desert, or food that angels brought to her.

This is the way to tell the difference in the paintings of Hairy Mary – Mary Magdalene holds a jar of oil and Mary of Egypt holds three loaves of bread.

Notably, skulls are sacred to both Marys and appear in paintings of both Mary Magdalene and Mary of Egypt. Incidentally various branches of the Church, including

Eastern Orthodox, highly venerate St. Mary of Egypt, with the Catholic Church recognising her as a patron Saint of Penitents.

The Last Supper painting by Leonardo Da Vinci
The painting was started in 1495 and is a wall fresco in the Church of Santa Maria delle Grazie near Milan, Italy. It chronicles an event that appears in all four canonical gospels.

The evening before Jesus was betrayed, all the disciples got together to eat and drink with him, and Jesus informed them of his fate, and how to remember him once he was gone. Jesus washed their feet which was a way of letting them know they were under the protection of the Lord. The disciples look shocked and surprised in the painting, which depicts the few moments after he told them of the betrayal. There are twelve disciples, plus Jesus in this painting, and it is thought that this is another reason why the number thirteen is said to be unlucky.

Leonardo has painted himself into the painting, second from the right as St. Jude. Jesus is painted in the middle, with six disciples on his left side, and six on his right, showing Da Vinci's love of symmetry.

In the place of honour, on Jesus's right side, is a feminine-looking person with flowing red hair, wearing a necklace, and posing in a demure manner. This feminine character and Jesus are sitting in a mirror image of each other. Even their clothes are co-ordinated; he wears a blue robe and red cloak, and she wears a red robe and blue cloak, in the same style, two halves making a whole maybe? They are portrayed as being joined at the hip, leaning away to create a negative space between forming a V chalice and an M for Mary or Magdalene. The centre of the painting is slightly misplaced to the left, at odds with Da Vinci's usual symmetry.

The left is usually seen as the feminine side, energetically, spiritually and emotionally.

St. Peter, the founder of the Church of Rome, is known to be jealous of Mary, and as such is mentioned many times in the Gnostic Gospels. His hands are in a menacing gesture which could be interpreted as a blade at her neck. There is also what has been interpreted to be a disembodied hand pointing a dagger towards the stomach area of the third disciple from the left. The Church maintains that figure is the disciple John who is always placed at Jesus's right hand. In The Gospel of St.

John, he is described as leaning on the bosom of the Lord during the occasion of the Last Supper, yet here he is shown as leaning away? He is depicted in Da Vinci's other painting *Saint John the Baptist* as a young man with long hair and feminine features.

Leonardo was fond of painting feminine-looking male characters, so it could even be a combination of both Mary and John. It is unclear who this character is in the painting next to Jesus, and theories abound about whether it is John or in fact Mary Magdalene.

The Grail Mysteries
The grail romance poems were essentially Pagan, based around nature, seasonal cycles and the cycle of rebirth. The earliest appeared in the 12th to 13th century from the Court of the Count of Champagne, who incidentally is thought to have been one of the founders of the Knights Templar.

The first Grail romance was *Le Roman de Perceval*, also known as *Le Conte du Graal*, written by Chrétien de Troyes, forming a prototype for other grail stories to be based on. Set during King Arthur's reign, Percival leaves home in search of a knighthood. He spends the night in a castle at the request of a fisherman.

The grail makes an appearance as a jewel-encrusted golden dish carried by a lady, but it is not clear what the grail actually is, nor are any links to Jesus or Mary mentioned. As Percival doesn't ask the right questions of the grail carrier, he awakens to an empty castle and finds great tragedies happening in the world. Percival discovers he is part of the Family of the Grail and because of the problems since meeting up with the grail, he declares that he no longer loves God.

This text is open to multiple interpretations and was either unfinished or parts of it were lost over the years. It was only during later stories that the grail was linked to King Arthur and Jesus.

Roman de l'estoire dou Saint Graal was written by Robert de Boron between 1190 and 1199. Here he tells the story of the cup being drunk from at the Last Supper and later used by Joseph of Arimathea to collect the blood of Jesus during the crucifixion, and this blood giving the grail magical powers. Galahad is said to be Joseph of Arimathea's son, but it is not mentioned to be set in the times of King Arthur.

The stories lost popularity for about two hundred years but saw a revival by Sir Thomas Malory in 1470 with his work called *Le Morte d'Arthur*, and have been popular ever since.

The Da Vinci Code book by Dan Brown
This fictional book centres on the existence of holy bloodline descendants directly from Jesus and Mary Magdalene. The line of descent being carried through the Merovingian French kings who had the surnames Plantard and Saint Clair.

These names have a long history through the Merovingians and the Knights Templar. The book suggests that the holy grail is in fact this bloodline, and alludes to the bones of Mary, or the secret documents about the bloodline, being hidden under the Louvre, where the inverted crystal pyramid is over a small upright pyramid. The book is heavy on symbolism, including the Star of David (Solomon's Seal), which when joined together, represents the male and female, in the form of the blade, an upright triangle and a downward triangle forming the chalice.

The secret of the holy grail bloodline was protected by the Priory of Sion throughout history, with Leonardo Da Vinci being listed as one of the Grandmasters of the Priory. The Priory was said to have had great respect for the divine feminine and the goddess. Four of their grandmasters were female, and their military arm was the Knights Templar. The Priory also believed that powerful men in the Church spread lies about the divine feminine's role in history, tipping the scales in favour of the masculine. Emperor Constantine played a large part, with his campaign of propaganda and the removal of gospels which did not serve his patriarchal purpose, so he removed the role of the strong feminine from the Biblical texts. This was believed by the Priory to have left the world out of balance, causing wars and a disrespect for Mother Earth, and that when the time was right the documents proving the holy bloodline would be released into the world, but that had not yet happened.

Although this is a fictional book, some readers take this as gospel truth and think that the story is real and that the Church, the Vatican or a secret order are in possession of the documents.

The Mary Magdalene movie 2018
This film stars Rooney Mara as Mary and Joaquin Phoenix as Jesus. It stays faithful to the Biblical narrative and is clearly written to appease the Church. It is beautifully made, and although it was clear in the movie that Mary and Jesus had great love and respect for each other, it showed that they were not married or in a relationship.

This is in direct contrast to *The Last Temptation of Christ*,[8] which the Church tried to ban as it depicted Mary and Jesus in a sexual relationship, and departed from the gospels.

The only tiny bit that I could see in the *Mary Magdalene* movie that comes from the Gospel of Mary was right at the end after Mary was questioned by Peter about the appearance of Christ after his crucifixion. The disciples had expected the world to change and that is why Judas betrayed Jesus to the Romans. Mary explained the changes were within us, and that we are the kingdom, which is a clear message of the Gospel of Mary.

Tarot
Margaret Starbird has written about Tarot and how it links into Mary's story. Tarot is based on a medieval Italian card game that was full of hidden symbolism, and it was a secret way of passing along ideologies banned by the Church. These are some of the links in brief from the Charles VI deck.

Cups/chalice: A symbol of the feminine and the womb, the sacred waters, and the holder of secrets. In tarot represents the element of water.

---

[8] The Last temptation of Christ is a 1988 film directed by Martin Scorsese. It stars Willem Dafoe as Jesus and Barbara Hershey as Mary Magdalene. https://en.wikipedia.org/wiki/The_Last_Temptation_of_Christ_(film)

Wands: A symbol of the sprouting rod of Joseph of Arimathea and representative of the royal line as well as representing energy and action. Wands represent the element of fire.

Swords: A masculine symbol, phallic and representative of the swords of the Knights Templar. Swords signify the element of air in tarot.

Pentacles/plate: A grail symbol, and a symbol of the divine feminine and the Goddess, and the element of earth, grounding and stability.

Ace of Cups: A symbol of sacred union with the bowl representing the womb and the stem of the phallus.

The Fool: A travelling troubadour recounting the tales of The Lady. The dog at his feet represents the Catholic Church.

The High Priestess: A lady with arms outstretched, just like the goddess, Isis, is depicted.

A reference to Mary in her role as a High Priestess of Isis. A feminine card.

The Lovers: Represent Mary and Jesus and the procession behind them (on some cards) represents the descendants of the Holy bloodline. Margaret Starbird said the original name for the card was The Vine. [9]

The Charioteer: A Templar returning with the spoils of war.

Strength: The symbolic strength of Mary. The lion – is it the Lion of Judah?

The Hermit: Peter the Hermit, who at the end of the 11th Century travelled from town to town drumming up support for the Crusaders to win Jerusalem back from the Saracens. The large rock formation at the side stood for Peter the Rock.

The Tower: Magdala means watchtower, so this could symbolise the tower falling under attack from the Church, and could also be the tower of strength. It is the spirit faced with destruction.

The World: Feminine sovereignty, Goddess, the spirit that has left the world behind. [10]

---

[9] Margaret Starbird is discussing the Charles VI deck. It is the fourth card pictured here.https://tarot-heritage.com/from-trionfi-to-majorarcana/lamore-lamoreux-the-lovers/

[10] For more information on the tarot correspondences, please see Margaret Starbird's books The Goddess in the Gospels and The Woman with the Alabaster Jar.

CHAPTER 10
THE MAGDALENE LAUNDRIES

Near a lovely magnolia tree in the centre of St. Stephens Green in Dublin, there is a plaque on a wooden bench with faceless heads on it, which reads, "To the women who worked in the Magdalene laundry institutions and to the children born to some members of those communities – reflect here upon their lives".

The bench is there to commemorate the lives of women who had been placed in the laundries because they had dared to have sex or become pregnant outside of marriage.

Some of the women sent there were judged by priests to have been in moral danger – including something as innocent as having no father figure, or going to the cinema with a man, which was enough to get you thrown into one of these hideous places.

These laundries existed as a form of extreme punishment, whose purpose seemed to be to break any spirit or free will the women had left in them and take any remaining power away from them. They were locked away, behind high walls, under Police guard.

The laundries were run by orders of nuns, who were known to be cruel to the poor women in their care. Simple things brought out the nuns' wrath and incurred a beating. Heaven forbid you would drop a spoon. The women wore unkempt clothes and used dented tin crockery, but when the inspectors came, out came the best china and clothing, only to be taken away afterwards.

Life in the laundries was harsh, with long hours and backbreaking work right up to childbirth. The women, who were known as Maggies, lived in fear of getting beaten, or even tortured, for very minor misdemeanours by the Sisters of Mercy.

The Maggies were given new names on entering the laundries and a number of the girls were told that their families had moved away, abandoning them and making it impossible for them to get in contact with family members. To top it all, if in fact it could get any worse, the babies were taken away and many were sold to wealthy Americans, never to be seen by their mothers again.

The laundries were based mainly in Ireland, but there was also one in Edinburgh. There are two shocking things here. Firstly, the name Magdalene was obviously used as in their eyes she was a penitent prostitute – the ultimate fallen woman – and secondly, the fact that the last one closed in 1996. Yes, 1996.

"Why has thou forsaken me?"
Matt. 27: 46

CHAPTER 11
MY OWN EXPERIENCES WITH MARY

Whenever I am in need of divine inspiration or wisdom, Mary is my first port of call. I meditate if I don't have much time, or do the pathworking, which I have detailed at the end of this book, if time allows. I wrote the pathworking especially to make contact with her. Sometimes I don't even need to reach out to her – I think of a problem I have, and Mary pops into my head with her pearls of wisdom or even offers me a solution. And she has a very high success rate with her ideas.

In November 2020, when I was a few months into my training journey with the Fellowship of Isis Goddess training, I went away for the weekend with my husband. I was at the point in my training where I had to focus on three Goddesses to work with but at that time, I had not found the right Goddesses for me. I was reading the training materials and applying the daily practices but at that time I was a bit lost, spiritually, so I decided I needed to go on a trip to be closer to nature and we chose to visit a beach. We travelled in our motorhome to the South coast of Carmarthenshire.

After an exhausting walk up a hill to Llansteffan Castle, I was decidedly slower on the way back down. I stopped on the pebbled beach and looked down to see two particular stones which stood out to me. The first was a rectangular stone with a clear indented area in the shape of a face. It had very clear features and, even now, some days I look at it and it looks like Medusa with her snake hair and other times it looks like Jesus with a crown of thorns. The second stone is the most interesting and sacred to me. It fits perfectly in my hand, a long narrow figurine-shaped stone. It looks like a lady with a veil partly across her face.

The light rain seems to give a form to the stones, highlighting their features, especially the Medusa stone. When the stones are dry the features are barely visible – if it had been a dry day, I am not sure I would have noticed the stones at all. I hold the Mary stone in my hand sometimes, when I particularly want to link in with Mary's wisdom.

The stones sit on my shrines, the Mary stone on my dedicated Mary shrine and the Medusa stone on my general Goddess one. One day I will research Medusa and see why she called out to me.

Around 2020–21, I kept getting a clear vision popping into my head at random times, with increasing frequency, in both my dreams and daydreams. I knew this image was not going to leave me until I had committed it to canvas. No mean feat as I am not an artist and have never painted beyond the primary school level. The vision consisted of an enormous wooden cross, with glowing rays manifesting from it, coming out of the top of St. Michaels Tower on Glastonbury Tor. The centre of the cross was decorated with massive red roses in full bloom. The rose petals were slowly shedding and falling down through the centre of the tower and were visible through the open arches. The petals start to flow down spiral pathways looping around the Tor, and gradually on the way down, the petals turn into drops of blood and are collected in a glowing chalice at the bottom.

As I look at this painting, I see many things going on, at different levels.

I feel tears shed for a lost love. Blood shedding from the holy womb. The rose petals of secrets kept falling and tumbling away. The holy bloodline. Patriarchal involvement in matriarchal ancestral wounds. Links to the Tor and the holy grail. Did Jesus visit Glastonbury? The list goes on with the meanings I have found in this powerful image.

A Vision from the Heart

In 2022 I was offered the chance, via a friend, to help staff a pop-up Goddess Temple at the Fantasy Forest festival. It was a busy festival, and the Goddess Temple was a popular outpost, offering tarot readings and reiki outside in the sunshine. I worked inside the temple, counselling, supporting festival goers and offering oracle card readings for free, or donation only. I had never picked up an oracle card at that time, let alone given readings. I am not heavily into divination; I am more of a spell worker. There was a basket with several different decks in it, and visitors were able to choose which one appealed to them. Every single person I read for chose the same deck, *The Divine Feminine Oracle*, based around its imagery, which had the look and feel of the Magdalene. Here is where it gets a bit strange. I let people choose 1–3 cards and gave a reading. Only I didn't give a reading at all. The messages came straight from Mary herself. I saw her in my mind's eye and repeated what she said to me. I didn't refer to the book at all, I didn't need to. And the feedback – I had people in tears telling me how accurate it was and how much the messages meant to them and the guidance I gave. The first thing I did when I got home was to buy the oracle cards myself, but this time I had to read the book, as Mary is not currently looking over my shoulder as the cards are drawn. I think it was a special time and place, and the cards aligned with my divine feminine link that day.

Summer of 2022, I was at another well-known Pagan camp and a holy grail ritual was led by a very famous witch. I noticed a few things during the ritual. There was definitely an unaccounted-for presence in the room. As I watched the lady leading the ritual, her face darkened and changed slightly, momentarily. I was not the only person to notice this. A large amount of energy was raised and directed towards a chalice, which shimmered and the fluid inside rippled on the surface. Definitely an unusual experience.

In early 2023, I had been dabbling in trancework in a circle with the usual protections in place. I was trying to make contact with The Morrigan but something a bit more sinister showed itself to me instead.

With me in the circle was my husband. Normally, I am the one to take control of this kind of situation, but unfortunately, as I was on the receiving end of this entity, my husband had to take charge. He said it was difficult and he was losing control and all the ways he tried to remove the entity were failing. A white misty figure with no features appeared behind me, in front of my husband. He had a strong feeling that it was Mary and she was protecting me. With this appearance, the entity started to retreat, and I started to come round to my husband explaining to me what had happened.

He had never had an experience like this before, and neither had I, nor have we since this episode.

Another strange experience happened to me in August 2023. My husband and I were away for the bank holiday weekend. We spent the day at Tatton Park, in Cheshire. A wet, miserable day for the most part, as the Summer of 2023 will mainly be remembered for. As usual, I was woefully underdressed for the weather and got drenched from head to toe visiting the gardens. So, we headed over to the house, mainly as a means to dry off. We had intended to visit the house, but much later in the day, as the main draw to visit Tatton Park for us was the gardens.

As I stepped over the threshold, into the main house, I had an image of Mary in my head and she said to me, 'Look for my image'. Tatton Park is full of original, beautiful paintings, many of them being religious in content. I walked through several rooms and spotted a few images which I thought looked like the Virgin Mother, but none specifically of the Magdalene. One of the volunteers, a few rooms into the house seemed to be knowledgeable about the paintings in the room she was in, so I asked her if there were any of Mary Magdalene in the house. She suggested that if there were any images of Mary, they would be on display in the Card Room, a few rooms back.

So, we headed backwards, against the natural flow of visitors and 'This Way' signs, and I explained to a volunteer, Ruth, that I was heading back to the Card Room to look for something. I looked all around the room, and all I could find that remotely fitted with the message was a painting of Joseph of Arimathea, which I took a photo of, who as I mentioned earlier, is entwined with Mary's story.

With this, I headed back to the room I had recently left and walked past Ruth again. She asked me if I had found what I was looking for. Here is where it gets strange. I told her about my message from Mary as I entered the house. She smiled and opened the huge binder she had on her lap, and the first page was filled with an image of a painting called *The Descent from the Cross* by Rogier Van Der Weyden, painted in the 15th Century. It features, amongst others, Jesus, Mother Mary and Mary Magdalene. It had been the subject of a BBC programme in 2010 and now hangs in the Museo del Prado in Madrid.

I took photos both of the image she had of the painting and also the description. Ruth had seen the Madrid painting and described the beauty of it but did not explain why she had the image in her file. It's only now that I have started to investigate the background of the painting and the reason she had it at the top of her file in Tatton Park. In the painting there is Joseph of Arimathea and Nicodemus, and the portrait of Joseph that I took a photo of, is a copy of the face from the masterpiece. That is why she had the image.

There is something unusual about this large painting. It was painted as a commercial commission from the Guild of Archers in Leuven to hang as an altarpiece in The Chapel of Archers at the Chapel of Our Lady Outside the Walls. To tie into the archery theme, there are two tiny images of crossbows in the corners, but also Jesus, Mother Mary and Mary Magdalene are painted in strange poses, resembling the curves of a bow. Once their unusual posture had been pointed out, it was clear to see. Mary Magdalene is painted on the far right of the image in a very strange stance, like a crossbow.

Descent from the Cross

At the end of August 2023 Mary was still very prominent in my life. I realised that the Coven I run had a name that could be attributed to Mary. It's not my name to give, as I didn't name it, so I won't name it here. It's a coven I took over from the previous High Priestess. I was looking for a new coven chalice, as the one I currently use is my own personal one. The one I bought fits in with the coven's name and it has Mary's vine on it. It was there, just waiting for me, once I put the message out into the universe that I was looking for a new coven chalice, one found its way to me. My coven now has a new name, one that I gave it, which is special and personal to me.

Fast forward to the September 2023 full moon, vine moon esbat ritual. Probably not a coincidence that it was the vine moon, given the links with Mary and the vine. We had coven homemade wine, which is rich with vine fruit from our garden on the coven's land, and we did magical work with branches cut from the vine of the land. It was a few days past autumn equinox, and we had made more wine as part of the equinox ritual.

The vines I use can be seen as plants of balance, the fruit and the thorns co-existing together – a duality, male and female, so this time of year feels appropriate for the Magdalene energy.

I was the High Priestess and Mary came to me at an appropriate part of the ritual. My voice became softer, and I felt a gentler demeanour but was impatient with the High Priest, my husband, and prodded him with my wand and told him to step aside, as I wanted to speak. I delivered a combination of the ritual words I was meant to and words that flowed to me from deep within. The Magdalene energy remained with me for the duration of the ritual, slowly subsiding afterwards. Interestingly when I removed the circle with the sword, the coven group noticed the tip of the sword was glowing with an energetic red light.

I do multiple daily devotions of various types and as a consequence now feel that I have a unique link with Mary, one that I deeply treasure. She is my inspiration, a source of great wisdom and strength. Mary embodies feminine energy and I see her as a forerunner of feminism and a role model for independent women – the feminine face of empowerment. The Magdalene envelopes me in her strength and when I need advice, I sit with her meditating and she shares advice with me and guides me. In the following chapters are some of the techniques I use to draw her energy closer to me.

CHAPTER 12
PRACTICAL WORK

The path of the Magdalene is the path to inner knowing. She shows herself to people in different ways and your relationship with her is a deeply personal one. Mary will appear to you when you are ready to receive her, in a way unique to you. Open your heart, and she will come, she will guide you along the path, she is a source of great wisdom beyond our imagination. She can walk beside you during dark times too, when you are feeling lost, becoming your tower of strength, your own personal Magdala.

As a Priestess of Isis, trained in death rituals, she can be seen as a psychopomp, a guiding light when she is most needed, a supportive figure. She has suffered great loss and knows what the pain of despair feels like.
The Rose Path is never an easy one, the soft petals are in amongst the thorns, the good times alongside the trials of life.

It is a good idea to start a journal and record any messages or ideas that are given to you during these practical exercises. The journal will enable you to see any patterns that are forming in your deepening work with her. Decorate it with Magdalene imagery such as roses, the red egg, or the Camargue cross. Make a note immediately after the meditation work, before you forget any messages or inspiration that you have received. Keep the journal beside your bed as Mary has a habit of popping into your dreams once you have made it known to her that you are accepting of her wisdom and divine energy.

When you feel ready, create a shrine and fill it with her symbols such as roses, red eggs and pictures or statues of her. Use a red altar cloth with vines draped around it if you can. Maybe try scattering rose petals into the almond mandorla shape and set your statue of Mary inside it. Leave offerings on the shrine for Mary such as wine, water, fruit, and flowers and burn some incense.

If you can, make your own incense. I have included a recipe I use to make incense dedicated to Mary. If you are purchasing incense, it is possible to get Mary Magdalene blended incense, otherwise a rose mix, myrrh or Cathedral incense is a good choice. If you don't like incense, try a rose-scented perfume or room fragrance instead.

Burn a red candle whilst you do your devotions and affirmations, but don't burn a candle when meditating, due to safety, and never leave the flame unattended.

Use a nice chalice and pour red wine as offerings to her, or libate outside near a rose bush, a sacred well or vines. Keep an anointing oil on the shrine if you can, in a small jar, or dedicated dish. Paint icons and paintings, putting in your own personal energy into the items on your shrine. It's always a good idea to make as many of your magical or devotional tools as you can. Making them yourself you are putting your own unique energies into the tools, and you can make them exactly how you would like them to be.

I use veiling as a form of respect to Mary, as it was how females presented themselves in biblical times, and I sometimes wear a red veil to cover my hair. This is not essential, but it bonds me to her, makes the interaction between us more approachable and helps me get into the right state of mind for contacting Mary. In the same way that magicians put on their magical robes or jewellery to begin ritual or spell work, I put on the veil to shift me into consciously working with the essence of Mary Magdalene. Sometimes I put on my robe but it's not necessary. A red robe would be a good choice if you want to use magical wear, and sleeveless if you use lots of candles.

If you can, spend some time researching the historical Mary Magdalene. A good place to start is with Margaret Starbird. Try Pistis Sophia, although it is not the easiest of reads. The Gospel of Mary Magdalene, The Gospel of the Beloved Companion, The Song of Songs and the Gnostic Bible are essential reads on this journey, and if you want novels, look up Kathleen McGowan. Read the Grail Mysteries if you get the opportunity, as these link in with Mary visiting Glastonbury with Joseph of Arimathea.

Read as much history as you can, especially about the Cathars, the Merovingians and the Knights Templar, as her story is entwined with all these religious orders. If you are interested in the more modern way of working with Mary, that of portals, ascension codes etc, study the womb mysteries. These are the moon cycle and feminine life cycle-based mystery teachings, for which there are plenty of courses and books such as *Womb Awakening* by Bertrand and Bertrand.

Have you thought about training as a Death Doula? There are courses available that teach you the skills of a death doula. These skilled practitioners are also known as death or soul midwives. They work to support the terminally ill and dying, emotionally, spiritually, and holistically. Look up the work of the Myrrhophore and see that this links in well with the work of the death doulas. This could be done as a way of honouring Mary in her aspect as a Priestess of Isis doing the burial rites and rituals.

Honouring deities by working with an aspect of their whole being is one of the best ways of getting close to your Goddess and can be seen as a sacrifice for them, by giving up your time and money. On this subject, another way of working with Mary would be to study as much as you can, as Mary is the Goddess of wisdom.

When you feel ready, you may want to self-dedicate to her. You could write a short speech and light a candle, meditate and say your dedication. Make it heartfelt and personal to you, tell her what you would like from her and what in turn you would give to her as a sacrifice. A sacrifice does not mean that you have to chop a chicken's head off daily and spread the blood on her shrine, although you can if you want to, I am not here to judge. The sacrifice of time or money is just as good in my opinion. Free teaching, either one-to-one or in a group, working with the terminally ill, or giving money, in Mary's name to a cause that is close to your heart. Time and dedication are all that is required.

We each have individual journeys throughout our lives, one size doesn't fit all. After the dedication I am sure that Mary will show up in your life more, as you have formed a link with her. I made an oath of a lifetime of study and service towards the Goddess, and I don't intend to break that oath. One thing not yet mentioned, always remember to be respectful and thank Mary when you ask anything of her.

CHAPTER 13
MAGDALENE MYSTERIES AND NOVENAS

Traditionally, the mysteries are prayed on a rosary, but I have turned them into meditations and contemplations. They are the Magdalene's main stories and are a good place to start working with her. In brief, the mysteries are:

Mary having the seven demons chased out of her
Meditate on each of the seven chakras becoming cleansed and open.

Root: located at the base of your spine. Visualise a red lotus, slowly opening.

Sacral: just below your navel.
Visualise an orange lotus opening.

Solar Plexus: in your stomach area. Visualise a yellow lotus opening.

Heart: located at your heart centre. Visualise a green lotus opening.

Throat: located at your throat centre. Visualise a blue lotus opening.

Third Eye: on your forehead between your eyes. Visualise an indigo lotus opening.

Crown: on the top of your head.
Visualise a purple lotus opening.

Now imagine white light flowing down from the universe, through all your open chakras, from your Crown, down to your Root chakra.

When you feel refreshed and that your chakras are refilled and restored, close the lotuses, working in reverse from your crown to your root.

Mary, as a sacred priestess, would have learnt to use these techniques in the temple and would have done so in her myrrhophore work.

Opening these gateways enables a free flow of energy, a conduit throughout your body, purifying every part of your being.

Did Jesus perform a chakra cleanse on Mary, or was it a technique that she had learnt and taught to him?

Mary's tears over the death of her brother, Lazarus
Mary was distraught when her brother died and blamed Jesus for not being around to save him.

Contemplate the frustration she would have felt, and how she could resolve the feelings and switch them to feelings of forgiveness and relief when Lazarus was brought back from the dead.

Let go of any anger you may be holding inside.

Write down on paper something you want to release and let go of, and burn it.

Mary anoints the king
Meditate on this as being an initiation rite, a huge responsibility, and an intimate, sacred act. She pours the expensive oil over Jesus, becoming the Kingmaker.

Meditate on this special moment and feel the connection between the two of them.

Mary at the crucifixion
Meditate and feel her acceptance of the prophecy being fulfilled, even though she is personally filled with grief and horror. Imagine what it would feel like to be sat at the base of the cross, with Mother Mary and Mary of Clopas. You watch as your beloved has his life force

drained out from him. All you can do is watch and be there as support for him and his family, although you are tormented by what you see, and you feel so helpless.

Imagine the level of training it would take to hold him in her heart, to gaze at him with love, when all she probably wanted to do was to run somewhere, hide and cry.

Mary at the burial
Meditate on her role as a Priestess of Isis, preparing her beloved for his burial. Anointing him, performing the burial rites. The grief, the despair, the disbelief, although she knows it is her duty, and is what she has been trained for in the Temples of Isis.

Mary at the resurrection
Meditate on her shock at finding the grave empty, and then hearing the voice of her beloved call out to her. The shock turns to relief as she sees the vision before her, of her beloved Rabbouni.

Mary as the Apostle to the Apostles
Meditate on why she was chosen first to see the vision before her, and the enormous undertaking given to her of having to spread the word to the disciples. As Jesus proclaimed her as the one he loved the most, it is likely to be why he appeared before her, his beloved.

Contemplate on the injustice that Mary suffered, knowing she was the first to see the risen Christ, but she was rejected as being the first Apostle.

Mary in France
Meditate on Mary in her new role as the Divine Feminine source of wisdom, the teacher spreading the word of early Christianity, teaching in the cave in France and at various temples and religious sites around France.

Mary near death
As Mary nears death, visualise her in penance and prayer, being raised close to heaven by angels, soon to be reunited with her love, her other half, to become whole again. Completion.

Mary's legacy
Meditate on what you think Mary's lasting legacy is. The calling out to the Magdalenas. Is there a bloodline? The spreading of Christianity? Wisdom and knowledge? Divine sexuality and feminism rising up? There is the opposite side to this legacy, too – the Church was so fearful of her power and support that they hid her true story and tried to turn her into a powerless pitiful penitent woman.

So, the true story, her real legacy is coming forward, being brought out in the path being trodden by the Rose Priestesses.

Magdalene Novenas
A Novena is a series of prayers, meditations and readings that take place over the course of nine hours, nine days or nine weeks, broadly based on the mysteries detailed in the previous chapter.

The traditional way to work with the mysteries and the novenas is with rosary beads or prayer beads. If you would like to work with a rosary, but do not want a Catholic-themed one, there are guidelines online for making your own.

In the Catholic faith, St. Mary Magdalene's novena starts on July 13th and finishes on July 22nd, Mary's feast day.

The Catholic Novena set of prayer starts as follows, predictably:

> St Mary Magdalene, though you had committed many sins, you answered Christ's merciful invitation to you and became his devoted and beloved disciple.

Feel free to write your own versions of the mysteries or novenas. The mysteries are more of a mediative process and the novenas are devotional.

CHAPTER 14
VISUALISATIONS AND MEDITATIONS

The following meditations are not only good for building a relationship with Mary, but they are also an excellent practice tool for magical practitioners. These will help you experience the energies of the Magdalene. Try to practice one of them daily, until they become second nature to you, to the point where you can see the image in your mind's eye, easily, instantly, with your eyes open.

To change things up a bit, try using loose rose petals to form an almond-shaped mandorla on the ground to sit inside while you do your daily practices, and record any observations or thoughts into your rose journal.

My Daily Meditation
I anoint my forehead, and then put on my veil, if possible near my shrine, or I sit on the floor and make up a temporary shrine in front of me, remembering to make sure my cats are not in the room for candle safety.

Sometimes I burn incense or a candle if I can do so safely, then I close my eyes and visualize a white light, in my mind's eye.

I say a few words, these change on a daily basis. Something such as "Magdalene, divine light, share your wisdom, inspire me, guide me, on my path, today and always."

Mary usually steps forward into the light. She is usually radiant, dressed in red and although I can't see her features well, I just seem to know that it is her energy I can feel.

I open my mind and form a connection with her, just letting her communicate with me. She is my guide, my inspiration and she hasn't let me down yet.

The Egg
Close your eyes and imagine a cupped hand. What is it like? Old or young? Soft or rough? Skin tone? Painted Nails?

Nestled inside the hand is an egg. A plain, ordinary chicken egg. Visualise the egg slowly changing to red and hold this image as long as you can.

Open your eyes.

The Rose
Close your eyes. Visualise a red rosebud.

Imagine the scent from the rose. You could also burn rose incense, or use rose fragrance or use a fragranced anointing oil to help with the smell.

See the rose slowly opening, a petal at a time. When the rose is fully open, imagine the petals dropping one by one until they have all fallen.

With each petal falling, visualise something that you want to remove from your life dropping away and leaving with the petal, trusting Mary to assist you with this.

Another variation of this rose meditation is one that I teach in my magical group. Before you start, ask Mary Magdalene to give you a message during this meditation.

Close your eyes, imagine a rose bush. The roses are still in bud. Each of the roses are different colours.

Which colour rose are you drawn too? In your mind's eye, focus on the rose that calls to you, and slowly visualise the bud opening into full flower.

When the flower is fully open, there may be a gift inside, a message personal to you. It may be an item such as a feather or shell or an item of jewellery. The rose may be empty and the goddess may speak to you.

Always give the goddess thanks for your gift.

When you are ready, open your eyes.

Record any information in your journal. I would think about what the item inside the rose was, ponder over it, and try and work out what the message for you is.

The colour of the rose may be significant too. Colours have different meanings, and this will be part of the message.

The Blood Chalice
Close your eyes. Visualise a simple chalice.

How does it appear to you? Is it wooden? Stone? Hold it, and feel the weight of it in your hands.

The chalice is full of rosebuds. Smell them. Take one out and feel its velvety texture in between your fingers, rub it and smell the scent.

You look into the chalice. Slowly the petals wilt, and liquify. The smell of iron rises from the chalice, and you realize it now contains blood.

When you hold the chalice, what is the impression you get in your mind's eye from the blood? Is it the blood of Christ? The holy bloodline?

Meditate on this and visualise the blood being poured as an offering on the ground.

A plant grows from the soil. What is the plant? A rose with thorns? A vine symbolizing the Merovingians? Lily of the Valley, or one of the other flowers sacred to Mary?

Open your eyes.

Ponder on this meditation and make notes in your journal.

Magdalene image visualisation
Find an image or statue of Mary that resonates with you, as close to the way that you feel Mary would be represented. Find one with lots of symbology present, such as skulls, books, roses or a red egg in the image. Even better, create an image yourself channelling the divine energy into a painting, allowing the ink or paint to just flow. Explore your own creativity.

Look at the Magdalene image regularly, and notice all the signs and symbolism in the picture. Study it well until you can see the image clearly with your eyes closed.

Set up a small altar, with the image on it. Burn an incense that you feel is appropriate, but don't burn a candle as you will be meditating.

When ready, close your eyes, and see a light, flowing red veil in front of you.

Push it aside and step into the image you have memorised.

Look all around you. What do you see?

Walk up to Mary and ask her if she has a message for you.

Spend some time with her. Does she hand you a gift?

When you are ready, turn around and move back through the veil.

Open your eyes.

Be sure to make a note in your journal of any experiences you have had during the visualisation, and if appropriate research the meaning and the symbology of the gift you were given.

Christos and Magdalene Energy
This is an ideal exercise for two people, ideally in a loving partnership. One person to represent the Christos energy, and the other to represent the Magdalena energy.

Standing up, both of you face each other, holding both hands to form a circle, eyes closed.

Each of you visualise a beam of intense light coming straight down from the heavens, through your crown chakra, into your heart centre.

The person representing the Magdalena focuses on red energy, and the Christos focuses on blue.

When the energy enters into the heart centre, focus on the two light energies from each of you joining together to form an intense white light. Take a few moments here.

When ready, send the light energy through your left arm into your partner's right arm, receive the energy back through your right arm, then send it back across your heart centre and down your left arm again, so forming a circle of energy, a joining of energy. Two are becoming one.

When your energy sharing feels complete, earth it by sending the energy down into the ground to nourish and sustain the earth and the life contained therein.

Open your eyes, look into each other's eyes, and share a big, tight hug.

Anointing and Daily Affirmations
If you can, make yourself an anointing oil to use for your daily devotions. Spikenard is expensive, so it is acceptable to use patchouli, ylang ylang or a rose oil instead, or any of the nine sacred oils listed in the Myrrhophore section.

Always use a skin-safe base oil such as olive oil or sweet almond oil and add a few drops of your chosen aromatic.

Don't use undiluted essential oils directly onto the skin and if you are pregnant or if you have any other relevant medical conditions, check with your doctor to ensure that the essential oil is safe to use. Rosa Mystica is a beautiful blend of three types of roses, a white, a red and a pink.

Using rose-scented perfumes and toiletries daily will help keep you in the presence of this divine energy.

To use the anointing oil, dip your finger into the oil, and choose one of the following:

Anointing the King
Anoint your crown chakra with the words,
"I am the sovereign of my own life. I wear the crown of a queen/king/sovereign."

Acknowledging the wisdom within
Anoint your forehead (third eye) dabbing a small amount with your finger, and say,
"I am wise, the knowledge that I seek comes from within, I am worthy of manifesting a life of my choosing."

Wisdom
Anoint your throat area, and say,
"Words have power, I speak wisely but clearly and use my voice for only good and to utter sacred names."

Magdalena Love
Anoint your heart chakra and say,
"I am love, I feel the love of the divine Magdalene energy, deep within my heart and soul."

Mary holding her own against Peter
Anoint your solar plexus and say,
"I am confident, and can make decisions from a place of inner wisdom."

Divine Sexuality
Anoint your sacral womb / phallic area and say,
"I am a divine feminine/masculine/person. I hold an inner light within the seat of my soul, I am sensual and sexy and am worthy of love."

Christos Energy
Anoint your root chakra and say,
"I feel safe and secure and balanced, on this earthly journey."

Matriarchal Lineage
Anoint your feet and say,
"I walk the path of the sacred rose, I follow the wisdom of the ancestors."

Death Doula work
Using myrrh in olive oil, anoint someone you love in their last hours of life, and give them a heartfelt blessing that you have written yourself. Something personal that fits in with the belief system of the ill person, such as "may the loving arms of the divine encircle you, protect you and carry you on your journey to the next realm."

Whilst doing this, imagine Mary as a psychopomp beside them ready to help with their transition into the light.

Burn a myrrh-based incense if it feels appropriate and you are able to.

A white candle is a good choice here too, as a guiding light. Visualise Mary in her role as Priestess performing burial rites.

Intention here is important. Think carefully about the words you say, be a comforting presence. Only burn what is safe and comfortable for the person and surroundings.

CHAPTER 15
PATHWORKING TO VISIT MARY

A pathworking is a form of guided meditation, an inner journey usually with a purpose or a destination at the end. You can do a pathworking to visit a place, a point in history or the future, to communicate with a goddess or one of your guides, for example.

Ideally, get a trusted friend to read this meditation to you or make a recording yourself that you can play back.

Light some incense, maybe some myrrh, patchouli or rose, but not a candle for safety reasons.

Relax and follow the instructions. This pathworking will take you back to the time of Mary spreading her teachings in the cave at Sainte-Baume.

Get yourself in a comfortable, relaxed position. You can be sitting, or lying down if you prefer.

Close your eyes. You will keep them closed for the duration of the meditation.

Take some deep breaths. Breathe in through the nose, and out through the mouth. Feel your body becoming relaxed and light.

Relax back into normal breathing.

Imagine a white mist descending over you. Surrounding you, swirling around you, completely enveloping you.

[Pause]

Slowly the mist clears, and you are sitting on damp grass. You can feel the morning dew.

What are you wearing? Are you warm? Cold? Are your clothes from a modern time period, or from a time past?

The air feels fresh, and it is early in the day.

In the distance you can hear birds. Listen to the birds, and take in all the different bird songs.

You notice the scent of roses in the air. Stand up, follow the smell and in front of you is a rose bush. What colour is it? Pick a rose, smell it, and keep it with you.

You see a wellspring a short distance away from the roses, and the water gently trickles out, scoop your hands, catch some of the water, and drink some. Feel the coolness of the water in your hands and mouth.

In the distance you can hear a horse and cart trundling along a cobble road, gradually getting louder. Follow the sound, past the well and the rose bush and you come to a rough cobbled road.

In the distance is a large hill. The horse and cart get louder and louder until they reach where you are standing.

What does the horse look like? The driver of the cart? Who is it? Is it someone you recognise?

The horse stops and the driver beckons you to get onto the cart. What does he say? Is he silent?

You clamber onto the back of the cart. It smells musty and you appear to be sitting amongst old sacks. Shift into a comfortable position, hold on for the ride and lay back and take in nature all around you as you embark on your journey. Birds, trees, flowers, insects. Smells, sounds.

The journey is a bumpy one, with lots of twists and turns. You sense that you are going up a hill, and feel the jolts of the stones under the cart.

Sit up and look in the direction the cart is heading. You see a small opening in the side of the hill, a stone opening, a cave.

With this, the horse and cart stop, and you know the journey with the cart ends here.

Get off the cart and walk the last part of the journey yourself. The ground is uneven and every now and then a stone sticks into your foot. You know the path of a pilgrim is not always an easy one.

As you reach the entrance of the cave, you can hear a woman's voice, with gentle group laughter every now and then, and you know that this is where you are meant to be at this current point in time. Everything feels right and welcoming.

If you are wearing shoes, take them off outside the cave and slowly walk inside. It is slightly dark in the cave, and it is lit with candles.

As your eyes adjust, you can see a woman with olive-toned skin and dark hair partially covered in a red veil. She is wearing robes of red and is seated on a rock, higher up than everyone else.

You realise the room is not empty, although there is now silence and the group of people turn to see who their visitor is. Do you know any of these people? You get a feeling from them of welcoming acceptance as several smile at you and one beckons you over to sit by them.

The lady on the rock smiles at you and nods. You know that this lady, Mary Magdalene has great knowledge, and wisdom well beyond our comprehension. She is a teacher and the people surrounding her listening intently to her every word are her students.

She asks you if you have any questions for her. Take some time here to ask her any questions you might have and let her give you some answers.

[Long pause]

When you are ready to leave, walk up to her, give her he rose and thank her for her time and connection.

She accepts the rose and gives you a gift in return. The gift is personal and meaningful to you. What is the gift? Take some moments to look it over.

You hear the horse and cart returning. It is time to leave. Put your shoes back on and walk back down the hill feeling the rocks beneath your feet.

The air is fresh, and birds are flying around. An insect flies past. What insect is it? Do you see any other animals on your walk back to the cart?

You arrive at the cart and climb back on. With a nod to the driver, your journey down the hill starts.

The damp bags are gone and there is now fresh produce in the cart. Pick a piece of fruit or a vegetable up, smell it and feel the texture of it.

The cart jolts along on its journey back down the side of the hill.

The horse and cart stop and you get off the cart.

The scent of roses fills the air and you walk towards the rose bush.

You hear the water of the wellspring and head over to it and drink some more of its fresh water.

Hold the gift in your hands. If it feels the right thing to do, place it in the spring as an offering and a thank you to the Goddess. If it doesn't feel like the right thing to do, that is ok.

The grass is drier now, sit down on it. Imagine a white mist descending and swirling around you, enveloping you.

Once the mist has cleared, and when you are ready, open your eyes.

CHAPTER 16
CONCLUSION

The divine feminine role has had no place in society for more than two thousand years. We have to champion her, and search for her buried deep within ourselves. She is our safe place.

There seems to be a community of Magdalenas rising out of our consciousness, out of a patriarchal society and reviving the matriarchal lineages of the ancient priestesses. A reawakening. From the womb activators, and portal openers, to those who revere and are devoted to her. However you see her, there is a community of like-minded Magdalenas.

In the past, the priestesses were the Marys, now they are the Magdalenas. The towers, her towers of strength. The awakening is coming at the right time; the power of the feminine is empowering us to speak up, to stand up for what's right. As other movements such as MeToo, Black Lives Matter and the transgender community rise up to have their voices heard, we have to wonder if this empowerment is linked to the rise in the Magdalene energy. Her wisdom is trickling down through humanity.

The Gnostics use the term Anthropos, which means divine humans, to be fully awake as a human being, opening up and accepting the divine humanity inside us, the goal of knowing thyself. It is what is happening throughout those who devote themselves to the Magdalene. She is within all of us, we just need the courage to awaken her. Courage comes from the word couer, which is French for heart – we need the heart-felt love to have the courage to bring her into our lives. Finding the right balance, between divinity and humanity. Working with her as a channel to the divine feminine energy, she is initiating us onto the Magdalene pathway.

Mary was not just a follower of Jesus, but his equal. Here is a thought to take away from this; we have all heard of the second coming of Jesus but what if this raising of consciousness, of the awakening of the red rose energy is actually the second coming of his wife, Mary Magdalene? An uprising of women. A rebalance of the suppressed feminine energy with the divine masculine energy. In the words of my darling husband, it all started with the Spice Girls.

> For nothing is secret that will not be revealed, nor anything hidden that will not be known and come to light.
>
> Luke 8: 17

CHAPTER 17
RECIPES

Mary Magdalene Incense
I make and use this recipe when I meditate and want to link into Mary's energy. It is good to use when I have questions to ask, or when inspiration is needed.

Myrrh is used to clear out negative energy and helps with spiritual enlightenment. The rose, being sacred to Mary, is soothing and balancing to the emotions. Marigold flowers (Mary's gold), are healing, bringing creativity and helping to connect to the divine. Ylang-ylang enhances focus, and mood and amplifies sexual desire.

All these ingredients combined together will help enhance your connection to the Magdalena.

> 5 parts myrrh resin
> 4 parts dried rose petals
> 2 parts dried marigold petals
> 8 drops ylang-ylang essential oil

Add all the ingredients together into a mortar. Whilst grinding with the pestle, focus your intentions into the ingredients. What kind of work will you be doing with

Mary? Think of this whilst you grind. Say a chant or a prayer. Grind together but not too finely. Store in an airtight container. Use a pinch of incense on a smouldering charcoal disc.

Navette Cakes
Navette cakes are boat-shaped dry biscuit cakes that are eaten around the Marseille area. They are oval and are about 7–8cm long. The biscuit is said to be symbolic of the boat that brought Mary to the coast of Provence.

The navettes were originally flavoured with orange blossom, and are yeast free and can be stored for a long time. They are mainly eaten around Candlemas which is February 2nd. They form the shape of a mandorla, the centre of the vesica piscis.

Another theory of the origin of these cakes is that they are fertility symbols of the Earth Goddess. They are a dry rusk type of biscuit which we use as dunkers like biscotti. The flavour is good.

My son tested the recipes and they tasted lovely and lasted for a week, but they didn't hold the shape well during the testing process. But it's the taste that counts, isn't it?

600g plain flour
250g sugar
75g butter
3 eggs
Zest of 1 lemon
1 orange squeezed

Put the flour, sugar and lemon zest in a bowl together. Add the butter, eggs and orange juice together and mix into a firm dough.

Leave the dough in a warm place or at room temperature for one hour.

Break the dough into about 12–14 small balls. Form each ball into an oval, pinching either end to form a boat, and make a slit along the middle lengthways, but not all the way through.

Butter a baking tin or line with greaseproof paper and put them in.

Put aside for two hours.

Cook in a medium oven, at 180 degrees for about 20 minutes.

FURTHER READING

Mary Magdalene: Lost Goddess, Lost Gospels
Jan McDonald

This is the book that started my journey with the Magdalene. It was published in 2006 by Capall Bann publishing. Unfortunately this publishing house no longer exists, but if you can find it for a good price on the second hand market, it is well worth a read. Reverend McDonald, is now a Christian minister, but prior to this was a Pagan for many years. So this this book is written from a unique viewpoint. It is beautifully written, and flicking through the book now, it has called me to read it again.

The Woman with the Alabaster Jar
Margaret Starbird

Margaret Starbird and Lynne Picknett's books on the Magdalene have influenced me, especially *The Woman with the Alabaster Jar*. Ms Starbird is an authority on Mary's hidden symbols and inspired me to research into these more deeply. Her study on the tarot and its links to the Magdalene/holy grail stories is extensive. One of the best books on the Magdalene, especially illustrating how the church picked and chose the story narrative and teachings via the gospels.

The Goddess in the Gospels: Reclaiming the Sacred Feminine
Margaret Starbird
This book describes Ms Starbird's own personal journey and her deepening study of the divine feminine and the New Testament through her research into the marriage of Mary and Jesus. She explores Gematria, which is coding of the Greek alphabet though number and numerical patterns. A good read if you want to develop your own relationship with Mary Magdalene.

Mary Magdalene: Christianity's Hidden Goddess
Lynn Picknett
I loved this book, but it isn't really a book solely on Mary. There is a large focus on Jesus and John the Baptist, and shows how the story of these three intertwine. Good if you want to understand the many layers behind the people.

The Gospel of Mary of Magdala: Jesus and the First Woman Apostle
Karen L. King
This book contains the translation of the Gospel of Mary Magdalene that I have used in my research. It has photographs of the original parchments in it and an in-depth study of the meaning of each section of the gospel. An essential read.

Kathleen McGowan www.kathleenmcgowan.com
Kathleen McGowan is probably THE authority on Mary. She is an author of Magdalene themed novels, but if you are able to listen to her talk, she knows anything and everything about Mary.

The Dead Sea Scrolls
J.M. Allegro
If you would like to learn more about the Dead Sea scrolls, I can recommend this book published by Pelican. I have a 1957 reprint which I found at the back of a National Trust bookshop. It is very detailed, describing the finding of the scroll fragments, their historical settings both in antiquity and now, and a good description of the content of the scrolls and their comparison with biblical texts. There is a very clear description of the Essenes, their beliefs and even details of a nearby archaeological dig and the findings. If you can find a copy in a second hand bookshop or online you won't regret it.

Inside The Bible: A Guide to Understanding Each Book of the Bible
Kenneth A. Baker
This book condenses each of the 73 books of the bible down into a summary of the events, the timeframe the book was written and a bit about the author of each book. A good starting point if you want a summary of

the text without having to read the whole bible. A point to note though is that it is written from a Catholic point of view, nonetheless I found it invaluable for starting research as it provides a background to each chapter of the bible.

Magdalene Mysteries: The Left-Hand Path of the Feminine Christ
Azra Bertrand and Seren Bertrand
I absolutely adore this book and have re-read it many times. If you are interested in learning more about the Priestess titles or the Ghent altarpiece this is the book I recommend. It goes right back to the era of the Dragon Priestesses and covers every aspect of Mary Magdalene you could think of.

Womb Awakening: Initiatory Wisdom from the Creatrix of All Life
Azra Bertrand and Seren Bertrand
This book delves into the mysteries of the womb as a creatrix, and as a spiritual vessel. It traces the history of the lost ancient path, of the feminine mysteries, of working with the womb and moon via the Magdalene and similar archetypes.

The Gnostic Bible
Edited by Willis Barnstone and Marvin Meyer
This is the copy of the gnostic apocrypha that I use. It

has an in-depth analysis of each gospel text and is an essential read if you want to understand the early mystical Christianity of Jesus and Mary's teachings.

The Da Vinci Code
Dan Brown
I think this novel, although a work of fiction, has been well researched and although there are some assumptions made in the storyline, there is a lot of information enclosed. Explanations of Goddess worship, the symbolism of the pentagram for example. An enjoyable read, especially if you believe in the Magdalene blood line.

Beyond The Da Vinci Code
Rene Chandelle
Goes in depth into some of the theories and ideas put forward in the Da Vinci Code novel. If you enjoyed the novel and want to learn more about the Holy Grail, Opus Dei, Priory of Sion for example they are explored somewhat in this book.

Most larger National Trust properties sell second hand books to raise funds towards the property's upkeep. What I didn't know was that behind the scenes in some of the bookshops they have large collections or unpriced, unsorted or specialised books that they don't think will sell very well. I found that if I asked, they would bring out an unsorted plastic tub filled with history or religious books and let me have a good browse. This is how I have found some of the best non-fiction books that I have, so don't be afraid to smile and ask.

REFERENCES

Below is a comprehensive list of sources I have quoted and referenced whilst writing this book.

Printed References

Allegro, John Marco (1959). *The Dead Sea Scrolls.* Pelican. 1957

Barnstone, W. and Meyer, M.W. (2009). *The Gnostic Bible.* Boston: Shambhala Publications Inc.

Bertrand, S. (2020). *Magdalene mysteries: the left-hand path of the feminine Christ.* Rochester: Bear & Company.

Brown, D. (2006). *The Da Vinci code: a novel.* New York: Anchor Books.

Chandelle, René. (2006). *Beyond the Da Vinci Code: the book that solves the mystery.* Bounty Books.

de Boron, Robert. (1927). *Le roman de l'Estoire dou Graal.* France: Champion

de Quillan, Jehanne. (2010). *The Gospel of the Beloved Companion.* CreateSpace Independent Publishing.

de Troyes, Chrétien (n.d.). *Le roman de Perceval, ou, Le conte du Graal*.

de Voragine, Jacobus. (1941). *The Golden Legend*. Arno PR

King, K.L. (2003). *The Gospel of Mary of Magdala: Jesus and the first woman apostle*. Santa Rosa, Ca: Polebridge Press.

Malory, Sir Thomas. (1996). *Le Morte Darthur*. Wordsworth Editions.

Mead, G R S. (2008). *Pistis Sophia*. Charleston, S.C.: Bibliobazaar.

Starbird, M. (1993). *The Woman with the Alabaster Jar*. Bear & Company.

Starbird, M. (1998). *The Goddess in the Gospels*. Simon and Schuster.

Watterson, M. (2018). *The Divine Feminine Oracle*. Hay House Inc.

ONLINE BIBLICAL REFERENCES

The Gospel of Jesus's Wife. (2016). [online]. Available at: https://hwpi.harvard.edu/hds-papyrus/home.

Maurus, R. *De laudibus Sanctae Crucis.* https://digi.vatlib.it/view/MSS_Reg.lat.124

New King James Bible. (2015). [online] Available at: http://biblegateway.com.

The Gospel of Mary | Mary Magdalene. [online] Available at: http://thegospelofmary.org

The Mishnah, Talmud, and Midrash Jewish texts. Documentaries on the Nag Hammadi texts, Dead Sea Scrolls and Gnostic Gospels on PBS channel and the History documentary channel

The Emerald Tablets of Thoth

Paintings Referred to in the book
Birago, Giovanni Pietro. *St. Mary Magdalene*, 1490. Sforza Hours illuminated book, the British Library, London.

Bouts, Albert. *The Head of Nicodemus in Prayer*, 1500. Hangs in Tatton Park, Cheshire, National Trust.

Bouts, Albert . *The Head of Saint Joseph of Arimathea in Prayer*, 1500.Hangs in Tatton Park, Cheshire, National Trust.

Caravaggio, Michelangelo Merisi da. *Martha and Mary Magdalene*, 1598.Also known as Martha Reproving Mary, The Conversion of the Magdalene and the Alzaga Caravaggio. In the Detroit Institute of Arts.

con Meditazioni, Rosario. *Jesus and Mary*, 1308. St. Jean Cap Ferrat, France.

Da Vinci, Leonardo. *The Last Supper*, 1495. Wall mural in Church of Santa Maria delle Grazie, Milan.

Da Vinci, Leonardo. *St. John the Baptist*, 1513. Leonardo's final painting, The Louvre, Paris.

de La Tour, Georges. *Magdalene with the Smoking Flame*, 1640.Two versions exist, one in the Louvre, Paris, the other in The Los Angeles County Museum of Art.

Fetti (Feti), Domenico. *The Repentant St. Mary Magdalene*, 1619.Galleria Doria Pamphilj, Rome.

Kelly, Fleur. *The Exorcism of St. Mary Magdalene*, 2010.
Part of a mural depicting Saints. St. Patrick's Chapel, Glastonbury Abbey.

Titian. *The Penitent Magdalene*, 1560.
The Hermitage Museum, Saint Petersburg, Russia.

van der Weyden, Rogier. *The Descent from the Cross*, 1435.
Museo del Prado, Madrid.

van Eyck, Hubert & Jan. *The Adoration of the Mystic Lamb*, 1432.

Also known as the Ghent Altarpiece, St Bavo's Cathedral, Belgium.

IMAGES FEATURED

Page 2
Camargue cross
Public Domain

Page 9
Mary as a Priestess of Isis
Claire Pingel

Page 14
The Lions head fountain at the Chalice Well
Laika ac from UK, CC BY-SA 2.0
<https://creativecommons.org/licenses/by-sa/2.0>, via Wikimedia Commons

Page 15
Chapelle du St Pilon.
Anthospace, CC BY-
https://creativecommons.org/licenses/by-sa/3.0>, via Wikimedia Commons

Page 17
The Reliquary housing Mary Magdalene's skull
Enciclopedia1993, CC BY-SA 4.0
<https://creativecommons.org/licenses/by-sa/4.0>, via Wikimedia Commons

Page 22
Fleur de Lis
Public Domain

Flower of Life
Public Domain

Page 23
Statue in the Basilique de Sainte Maire Madeleine
Chabe01, CC BY-SA 4.0
<https://creativecommons.org/licenses/by-sa/4.0>, via Wikimedia Commons

Page 25
Sarah La Kali black Madonna
Kaho Mitsuki, Public domain, via Wikimedia Commons

Page 28
The Goddess Mary Magdelene
Claire Pingel

Page 30
The entrance to the cave
Bjs, CC BY-SA 4.0
<https://creativecommons.org/licenses/by-sa/4.0>, via Wikimedia Commons

Inside the cave
No machine-readable author provided. Disdero assumed (based on copyright claims)., CC BY-SA 3.0 <http://creativecommons.org/licenses/by-sa/3.0/>, via Wikimedia Commons

The cave of eggs
Philippe COSENTINO, CC BY-SA 3.0 <https://creativecommons.org/licenses/by-sa/3.0>, via Wikimedia Commons

Page 33
A Crusader Knight
Marcelo.AFerr, CC BY-SA 4.0 <https://creativecommons.org/licenses/by-sa/4.0>, via Wikimedia Commons

Page 85
Horizontal Vesica piscis
Public Domain

Vertical Vesica Piscis
Public Domain

Page 101
Gun Salute to Honour Mary Magdalene
Itto Ogami

Page 106
The Penitent Magdalene
Georges de La Tour, CC0, via Wikimedia Commons

Page 107
The Sacred Egg of Mary Magdalene
Claire Pingel

Page 108
Venus in Transit
Public Domain

Page 126
St Mary Magdalene, Sforza Hours
Giovanni Pietro Birago

Page 142
A Vision from the Heart
Claire Pingel

Page 216
Descent from the Cross (Deposition of Christ)
Rogier van der Weyden, Public domain, via Wikimedia Commons

Claire Pingel is a Priestess of Mary Magdalene, a Wiccan High Priestess and Archdruidess.

She has written regular columns for her local newspaper and had articles published in specialty magazines.

More recently she has written a popular diploma course for an online college.

Claire is a regular speaker at moots, Pagan camps and online communities.

www.ingramcontent.com/pod-product-compliance
Lightning Source LLC
Chambersburg PA
CBHW070425120526
44590CB00014B/1537